THE LIFE OF PAUL
FOR TODAY

Also Available in the For Today Series:

The Apostles' Creed for Today by Justo L. González
The Beatitudes for Today by James C. Howell
Christian Prayer for Today by Martha L. Moore-Keish
Hymns for Today by Brian Wren
The Life of Jesus for Today by Ronald J. Allen
The Lord's Prayer for Today by William J. Carl III
Old Testament Prophets for Today by Carolyn J. Sharp
The Parables for Today by Alyce M. McKenzie
The Psalms for Today by Beth LaNeel Tanner
The Ten Commandments for Today by Walter J. Harrelson

THE LIFE OF PAUL
FOR TODAY

Lyle D. Vander Broek

WESTMINSTER
JOHN KNOX PRESS
LOUISVILLE · KENTUCKY

First edition
Published by Westminster John Knox Press
Louisville, Kentucky

10 11 12 13 14 15 16 17 18 19—10 9 8 7 6 5 4 3 2 1

Book design by Sharon Adams
Cover design by Eric Walljasper, Minneapolis, MN

Library of Congress Cataloging-in-Publication Data

Vander Broek, Lyle D.
  The life of Paul for today / Lyle D. Vander Broek.
    p. cm.—(For today series)
  Includes bibliographical references.
  ISBN 978-0-664-23186-6 (alk. paper)
  1. Paul, the Apostle, Saint.   I. Title.
  BS2506.3.V36 2010
  225.9'2—dc22
  [B]
                                        2009033749

PRINTED IN THE UNITED STATES OF AMERICA

⊗ The paper used in this publication meets the minimum requirements of the American National Standard for Information Sciences—Permanence of Paper for Printed Library Materials, ANSI Z39.48-1992.

Westminster John Knox Press advocates the responsible use of our natural resources. The text paper of this book is made from 30% postconsumer waste.

Dedicated to our children

Matthew Troy Vander Broek
and
Nathan Scott Vander Broek

Loving sons who continue to mentor me in the ways of fatherhood

Contents

Series Introduction   ix

 1. Introduction   1

 2. Paul before His Call   10

 3. Paul's Conversion and Call   20

 4. Paul's Early Steps as a Missionary   28

 5. The First Missionary Journey   38

 6. The Jerusalem Council   47

 7. Paul's Second Missionary Journey   58

 8. Paul's Third Missionary Journey   68

 9. Arrested in Jerusalem and Imprisoned in Caesarea   78

10. On to Rome   91

11. Paul as a Resource for the Christian Life   102

Appendix: A Pauline Chronology   105

Notes   107

Further Reading   111

Series Introduction

*T*he For Today series is intended to provide reliable and accessible resources for the study of important biblical texts, theological documents, and Christian practices. The series is written by experts who are committed to making the results of their studies available to those with no particular biblical or theological training. The goal is to provide an engaging means to study texts and practices that are familiar to laity in churches. The authors are all committed to the importance of their topics and to communicating the significance of their understandings to a wide audience. The emphasis is not only on what these subjects have meant in the past but also on their value in the present—"For Today."

Our hope is that the books in this series will find eager readers in churches, particularly in the context of education classes. The authors are educators and pastors who wish to engage church laity in the issues raised by their topics. They seek to provide guidance for learning, for nurture, and for growth in Christian experience.

To enhance the educational usefulness of these volumes, Questions for Discussion are included at the end of each chapter.

We hope the books in this series will be important resources to enhance Christian faith and life.

The Publisher

1

Introduction

Paul—A Best-Kept Secret in the Modern Church

What are your favorite parts of the New Testament? Where do you turn for spiritual nourishment and Christian knowledge? What New Testament book in your Bible has the most dog-eared pages, the most marginal notes, and the most coffee stains? How you answer these questions reveals as much about you and your church as it does about the usefulness of the New Testament book or author you have chosen.

I regularly pose this question to students in the class New Testament Introduction at the Presbyterian (U.S.A.) seminary where I have taught for the last twenty-five years. Most of these mainstream Presbyterians and Methodists answer by naming one or more of the Gospels. Surely this is no surprise. My guess is that Christians during most periods of church history would have answered the same. What is surprising is how few of these future pastors put those parts of the New Testament that deal with Paul and his teachings near the top of their list. The Bibles my students carry to class don't have many coffee stains in the latter half of Acts, nor do letters like Romans and Galatians show the telltale signs of heavy use. There are many reasons for this. Would-be Bible students in both seminary and church often tell me that they find Paul's Letters difficult to understand (not a new assessment; see 2 Pet. 3:15–16) and that this view of the accessibility of Paul affects how seriously they take the story of the apostle in Acts. More alarming, in my opinion, is a negative attitude toward Paul's thought. With little grasp of the context out of which Paul writes, Christians too often claim that Paul is arrogant, manipulative, and sexist. I am always amazed at the disconnect between our solemn affirmation of the authority of the Word of God and our easy critique and dismissal of Paul.

The life and teachings of Paul are incredibly underused by Christians in mainline churches. I can give many time-honored reasons why we need to rediscover Paul. The apostle is arguably the most important interpreter of Jesus Christ found in the New Testament (more than half of the New Testament is by him, said to be by him, or about him); some would say that he is the most significant theologian in the history of the church. Over the centuries many pivotal Christian thinkers have found their inspiration primarily in him: Augustine of Hippo, Martin Luther, John Calvin, and Karl Barth. And we as churchgoing Christians are necessarily influenced by Paul whether we recognize it or not. The words of institution used in our celebration of the Lord's Supper are usually drawn from Paul (1 Cor. 11:23–26). It is his words for "sin" and "salvation" that most often show up in our confessions (see Rom. 3:19–26). His images of Christian love (1 Cor. 13) and community (i.e., the body of Christ; 1 Cor. 12:12–27) define relationships in the church. Whenever Christians gather, the influence of this first-century missionary is unavoidable.

Still, in an era of diminishing loyalty to specific denominations or traditions, many will find the weight of Paul's past influence less than convincing. Perhaps a better way to encourage Christians to recognize this treasure in our midst is simply to point out how transformative Paul's interpretation of Christ can be in your present Christian walk. *Paul, in both his life and teachings, can shape your life as a disciple in amazing ways.* The Christ who is proclaimed by Paul can liberate and console and challenge. And let me make that more than a hypothetical possibility. I have seen Paul's influence change my students and my Christian friends. Even more, I know that Paul speaks powerfully today because he speaks to me. For me, the Christian life apart from his witness to Christ is unimaginable. Paul is indeed *for today*. If you are neglecting Paul, you are surely missing important ways your spirituality and your Christian discernment can be strengthened.

Four Important Ways Paul Will Speak to Your Christian Faith

What can you learn from Paul's life and teachings that will be vital for your Christian journey? Let me suggest four things. Although there is much debate about where the theological center of Paul lies,[1] the following are, in my opinion, the influences of Paul that can have the greatest impact upon the contemporary Christian life. According to Paul (and what we need to hear):

In Jesus Christ, God Seeks to Reestablish a Relationship with Us

Of course, the rest of the New Testament proclaims this message as well, although each writer emphasizes different aspects of it. Paul's special gift to us, I think, is that his life and preaching profoundly clarify two key parts of this message. First of all, Paul shows us *how* or *in what ways* people alienate themselves from God through their sin, whether it is defined as idolatry (Rom. 1:18–23), the abuse of religious traditions (Rom. 2:17–29; 3:27; Gal. 1:14; Phil. 3:4–9), or the most extreme kinds of hate of God and other humans (see the incredible list in Rom. 1:28–32). Second, Paul, more fully than any other New Testament writer, explains to us *how* God overcomes this alienation through the life and death of his Son, Jesus Christ. Paul uses a whole range of theological and relational word pictures to describe Christ's saving action (i.e., justification, redemption, blood sacrifice, in Rom. 3:21–26; reconciliation, in Rom. 5:6–11; life in Christ and the Spirit, in Rom. 8:1–17; etc.). Taken together, Paul's clear message about both the problem and the solution becomes a much-needed declaration of hope. Perhaps best of all, Paul lives this message. Changed by Christ from a persecutor of the church into a missionary, he is the best New Testament example of God's trans-formative power.

Our Transformation through Christ Shapes Us
into People Who Are Capable of Love
and Who Seek Christian Community

Paul emphasizes that we "have been taught by God to love *one another*" (1 Thess. 4:9, emphasis added). In the church, societal barriers that separate people, barriers of gender, race, or class, are left behind (Gal. 3:28). The Holy Spirit empowers us with gifts that build up the community (1 Cor. 12:7). Christians worship together and eat together (1 Cor. 14:26–33; 11:17–34). Acts shows Paul establishing specific congregations and working toward unity in the greater church. Paul's Letters themselves always emphasize the importance of relationships within congregations. The apostle cannot imagine Christians trying to live apart from the love and discipline found in the church.

As Transformed People, We Become Witnesses
to Our Salvation in Christ

According to Paul, Christians are people who are so changed that they cannot "contain" themselves. They *must* live righteous lives (Rom. 6:1–19). They *must* use their gifts for the Christian community (1 Cor. 12:4–14:40; see the next section). And although Paul can describe the mandate that Christians experience in many different ways, nothing is more important in his life and teachings than *mission* or our witness to Christ. Both in Acts and in Paul's Letters, we see that when Paul is confronted by the risen Christ, he is not only changed; he is also given the task of proclaiming the message of Christ (Acts 9:15; Gal. 1:16). As we look at the life of Paul, mission will be always and everywhere assumed.

God Continues to Work in the World
to Bring Salvation to All People

One of the most exciting messages of Acts and Paul's Letters is that God has a plan of salvation for the world. Over and over again, we will see how God leads people and shapes events in order to reconcile all of creation to himself (Rom. 8:18–25). God is not absent or impassive; God is intimately involved in the events of our lives and seeks our good. Contemporary Christians need to be able to see God at work in their world, and the life and writings of Paul witness powerfully to that involvement.

Responsible Readers

This book is one of many in the For Today series, a series designed to help mainline Christian laity rediscover important but underused (or misunderstood) resources for the Christian faith. Other titles include *The Beatitudes for Today*, *The Parables for Today*, *The Apostles' Creed for Today*,[2] and so on. The books are intended to be readable and relevant. I will do my best to avoid technical language, or if I think it needs to be used, to carefully define it. I will also do my best to show Paul's relevance for the contemporary church. This is a responsibility that I take very seriously.

But if you agree that both you and your church need to rediscover Paul, then *you*, as a reader of this book, shoulder a responsibility as well. If communication on this important topic is going to take place, then both you and I, both reader and writer, will need to apply ourselves. This encouragement to be diligent students of the Word grows out of years of teaching in adult classroom settings, mostly in Presbyterian (U.S.A.) and United Methodist churches, where many of the students came to class without doing their assigned reading, let alone thinking about it seriously. Have you had this experience? Our children are often far better prepared for church school than we are for Bible classes. As Christians, we are called to be responsible readers of those materials, especially the Bible, which build up our faith. Our lament about the declining use of the Bible in mainline churches rings hollow apart from our own and our congregation's serious study of the Word. Let me suggest several ways you can be perceptive students, both of this book and of the New Testament material that will serve as our source.

Read This Book with a Bible at Hand

The purpose of this book is to point beyond itself to the biblical text, God's authoritative Word for our lives. Ideally, you would read all of Acts and all of Paul's Letters before you begin. If this is too ambitious, make sure you read some of the texts in Acts and Paul referenced at the beginning of each chapter. Perhaps it would be wise to pick one biblical passage in each paragraph or section for more in-depth study. As you read it, ask yourself how it relates to the topic being discussed.

Read the Bible with Contextual Sensitivity

I could write at length about how to read the Bible, but let me here lift up two issues that have to do with context. First of all, always interpret a biblical passage in its *literary context*, how it relates to the book in which it is found. The second context important in biblical interpretation is that of the author and the author's community and world, what we often call *historical context*. What things about the situation of the author and his world need to be understood in order to grasp the meaning of the passage?

Good resources for these two types of contextual reading abound. For *historical* context, use a good New Testament introduction,[3] or simply use the introduction and notes in a good annotated Bible.[4] Any commentary will help with *literary* context, but nothing is more important than simply a willingness to read before and after your passage. Responsible reading in the Bible is like the approach we use in other books, although even more care should be taken because of the importance of the message.

Read this Book and Its Biblical References as a Spiritual Exercise

This small volume does not pretend to be a biography of Paul. The book's purpose is not simply to share information about Paul's life, but to show how Paul, in both his actions and words, can impact your Christian life. Take the time to read carefully. Prayerfully consider what God is saying to you through Paul. And I strongly encourage you to discuss the issues raised in this book in a group setting with other Christians. Use the questions at the end of each chapter to open the dialogue. Some of my best experiences of Christian community have come in Spirit-filled discussions of specific biblical texts. As you will see, Paul himself affirms that it is very difficult to grow as a

Christian without the affirmation and discipline that comes from the body, the church.

"Finding" Paul

You may be aware of what is called "the quest for the historical Jesus."[5] The canonical Gospels, Matthew, Mark, Luke, and John, were written a good many years after Jesus walked on earth (Mark, the earliest, was written about 70 CE), and they do not always agree on the details of Jesus' life and ministry. Since the eighteenth century, "finding" the historical Jesus has been an important topic in biblical studies. We as Christians cannot dismiss this issue. Although we *believe* the testimony of the Gospels concerning Jesus as the Christ, we must not ignore that he was a real historical being. Our faith is not built upon an idea or an attractive story, but upon the audacious assertion that God's Son became a human being and actually lived among us (John 1:14).

At first glance it may seem that "finding" the historical Paul could be easier than "finding" the historical Jesus. After all, we have no writings from Jesus' hand, but the church has preserved a large collection of letters written by Paul himself. Still, as anyone who has read Acts and Paul's Letters carefully will tell you, reconstructing a life of Paul presents its own set of difficulties. This book is not an academic "life" of Paul, and the following issues will not detain us a great deal, but I do think it is important for responsible Christian readers to be aware of some of the barriers that confront us when we study Paul.

Two difficulties will soon become obvious. First of all, Acts and Paul's Letters do not always agree on the details of Paul's life and teachings. When these tensions in our resources occur, we as modern Christians invariably want to ask, "What really happened?" Second, some of the New Testament letters attributed to Paul may not have been written by him.[6] How do you know what Paul said and did if not all of "his" Letters were actually penned by him?

In a book of this sort, I neither want to ignore nor overemphasize these issues. We have more, and more accurate, information about this lowly (from the world's perspective) Christian missionary than we do about many then-famous leaders of Paul's day. And the issues

I raise above do not mean that the gospel message is less than clear or compromised in some way. On the other hand, I think Christians do the Bible a disservice when they claim for it a kind of historical accuracy that would have been hard for the first-century mind to comprehend. The honest reader sees historical problems in the biblical text; they must not be simply dismissed. In the historical study of Paul, most scholars say that where the sources disagree, Paul's own letters typically trump Acts, and the undisputed letters trump those that may have been written later by someone else. I will employ this standard in my book. One of the hardest things for modern Christians to come to terms with is the reality that the infallible good news found in the Bible was written by normal, fallible human beings. This paradox will be an ongoing issue in our journey through Paul.

Our Game Plan

As you might guess, our study of Paul will be chronological, to the extent to which that is possible. Because Paul's own letters usually show only snippets of his life in relationship to a particular congregation, we will largely follow the outline of events found in Acts. Of course, the primary concern of Acts (and certainly Paul's Letters) is Paul's life *as a believer* and *as a missionary*, so that will be our primary focus as well. There are no biblical stories about Paul as a child or teenager, and Acts abruptly ends with Paul imprisoned in Rome. This rather incomplete picture of the historical Paul found in the Bible should not be a problem for you as a contemporary Christian, however. In fact, just the opposite is the case. As believers, our concern with the life of Paul *as it impacts our Christian lives* coincides exactly with the purpose of the biblical accounts.

We will begin with the pre-Christian Paul, and then spend a chapter on Paul's conversion/call. Several chapters will be devoted to Paul's missionary activity, noting pivotal events that mark his relationship both with congregations he founded and with the Jerusalem church. Finally, we will follow Paul to Rome and his imprisonment there, one that most likely led to his martyrdom. Join me in a serious study of the life and teachings of perhaps the greatest Christian missionary of all time.

Questions for Discussion

1. Are the life and teachings of Paul underused in your Christian life? In that of your church? Discuss the reasons for this and its impact.
2. How important is it to you that Acts and Paul's Letters do not always agree on historical details? Is it helpful for you to recall that Paul and the author of Acts were writing at quite different times and for quite different reasons?
3. Make a list of things you know about Paul's life. Compare your list to that of other members of your group. How would you assess your knowledge? Keep this list for comparison at the end of your study of Paul.

2

Paul before His Call

Biblical Texts: Acts 7:58–8:1; 22:3–5; 26:4–11; Romans 1:1–3:21, 7:4–25; Galatians 1:13–14; Philippians 3:2–11; 1 Timothy 1:15–17

The Few Details about Paul's Early Life

Paul, a Diaspora Pharisee

Compared with what we know about Paul's life and thought *after* he was confronted by the risen Christ, the New Testament reports little about the apostle's precall years. Even so, what is conveyed about Paul's early life is essential for our understanding of both how he was changed by Christ and how he responds to issues in the churches he has founded.

There is no biblical information about Paul's birth. Based upon the dating and sequencing of his letters,[1] it is probable that Paul's work as a missionary spanned the years 35–64 CE. The "young man" Paul who participated in the stoning of Stephen (Acts 7:58) may have been about twenty-five or thirty years of age. Assuming that Paul met the risen Christ shortly after this incident, we can speculate that he was born between 5 and 10 CE. Neither Acts nor Paul's Letters give any indication that Paul knew Jesus before his resurrection.

Acts states that Paul was from Tarsus, a city in the region of Cilicia in what is now southern Turkey (Acts 9:11, 30; 11:25; 21:39; 22:3). Acts also affirms that the apostle was "brought up in" Jerusalem and studied at the feet of the Pharisee Gamaliel

(Acts 22:3). In his letters Paul mentions neither Tarsus nor training in Jerusalem, but he strongly affirms his Jewish heritage (Phil. 3:5–6; 2 Cor. 11:22), and he does claim to be a Pharisee (Phil. 3:5). Paul's excellent Greek and ease with which he navigates the Gentile world support the idea that he is a Diaspora, or non-Palestinian, Jew. According to Acts (16:37; 22:25) Paul is a Roman citizen, a status used to his advantage on his missionary journeys (Acts 16:37–39; 22:26, 27).

In Paul's day it was common for Diaspora Jews to have both a Jewish name and a Gentile name. Acts calls the apostle "Saul" (Acts 7:58; 9:1; etc.; Paul's Letters do not mention the name) in its early narratives; then it shifts to the Greek "Paul" when his activity as a missionary to Gentiles makes that name more appropriate (Acts 13:9).

Like most Pharisees, Paul has a trade with which to support himself (see 1 Cor. 4:12; 1 Thess. 2:9). According to Acts 18:3, he has been trained as a "tentmaker" (one who works with leather or cloth), a term that now commonly refers to ministry supported by "secular" work. Unlike the typical Pharisee, Paul does not appear to have ever married. In 1 Cor. 7:7 the apostle actually speaks about his unmarried state as a gift from God.

Paul, a Zealous Persecutor of the Church

Above all, the early Paul is defined in the New Testament by his standing as a Jew and by his hostile relationship with an emerging group within Judaism called Christianity (for the origin of the term, see Acts 11:26). In fact, these two characteristics are often linked: Paul's status as a devout Jew and Pharisee is illustrated by the energy with which he persecutes Jewish Christians. Galatians 1:13–14 is a key passage. There Paul freely speaks about his "earlier life in Judaism," how he violently persecuted and tried to destroy God's church (1:13; see also 1:23 and 1 Cor. 15:9). At the time, these attacks on Jewish Christians confirmed in Paul's own mind that he was a "rising star" within the ranks of Jewish leadership (Gal. 1:14). As a defender of the faith, he proved himself to be "more zealous for the traditions of [his] ancestors" than his peers (1:14). This same logic is voiced in a speech by Paul in Acts 22:3–5. In this passage we are given more details about Paul's life as a persecutor of Jewish Christians. With warrants from the high priest and the council of elders in Jerusalem, Paul has been rounding up Jewish Christians, even those as far away as Damascus, and bringing them bound to Jerusalem to be imprisoned and sometimes killed (Acts 22:4–5; 9:1–2). But notice that here as well, Paul's motivation as an "enforcer" appears to have grown out of his self-assessment as a pious Jew: he was tutored at the "feet of Gamaliel," "educated strictly according to ancestral law," and "zealous for God" (Acts 22:3). Before he met the risen Christ on the road to Damascus, Paul was convinced that persecuting Christians was a way of doing God's will!

This, then, is the rather meager description of the early Paul. He was born a decade or so after Jesus was born. Although he originates in a Hellenistic city in Asia Minor and knows the Greco-Roman world well, he defines himself primarily as a pious, zealous Jew. More than any other characteristic of his early years, the New Testament describes him as a persecutor of the church. Paul sought to imprison and execute Jewish Christians because he felt that this new "Way" (Acts 9:2; 22:4; etc.) was a threat to the faith of his ancestors. Even before he met the risen Christ, Paul was bold and aggressive in his faith. He was a young man with connections to the Jewish establishment, distinguishing himself from his peers by his willingness to defend Judaism against the blasphemy of calling Jesus Christ the Son of God.

God's Plan for Saul

God Chose This Man?

In our next chapter I will describe what Paul believes is the last of Jesus Christ's resurrection appearances (1 Cor. 15:8), his self-revelation to Paul as he was on his way to Damascus to persecute Christians there. But it's important to remind ourselves about this radical conversion and call even now as we consider who Paul was before becoming a believer in Christ. We can only really understand the extent to which God changed Paul or employed his gifts if we know what kind of man Christ confronted on that road to Damascus. In Galatians 1:15–16 Paul says that his call, the revelation of God's Son and the mission that grows out of it, is part of God's design whereby he "set me apart before I was born." In what sense was the early Paul "set apart"? Does this mean that God was "grooming" Paul for his mission long before he met Christ? Why did God choose *this* man? Was Paul shaped for this important work, or did God select him in spite of who he was? What can we learn about the way God's plan is carried out by looking at the man that Acts calls Saul, a persecutor of the church who would become its greatest missionary?

An Obvious Choice

In many ways, the "pre-Christ" Paul is well suited to the call he would be given. He knows the Gentile, Hellenistic world well. His early years (at the very least) were spent in Tarsus, a major Greco-Roman city. Even if he moved at some point to study under Gamaliel in Jerusalem, his excellent Greek and fine rhetoric (see 1 Cor. 1:18–31 or Rom. 8:28–39) indicate that he received the "liberal" education of a Hellenistic youth. And as a young man, Paul had obviously learned not to be intimidated by the world around him. He is not afraid to use current means of travel (i.e., the wonderful system of Roman roads or by sea). He has the status and power of being a Roman citizen. Paul is at home in urban environments. Several passages in Acts and his letters indicate that he is well acquainted with pagan religions (1 Cor. 10:14–22; Rom. 1:18–32; Acts 17:16–34). Based upon what we know about his background, Paul's call to minister to the Gentiles comes as no surprise.

Nor are we surprised when God calls one who is a faithful, educated Jew. We modern Christians tend to forget that early Christianity was a group within Judaism. Jesus was a Jew, and his message of salvation was communicated through the spiritual language of Israel. Imagine how difficult it would have been to speak about Jesus, the messianic Jew, to Gentiles who had little or no knowledge of Jewish traditions. How does one speak about Messiah, Torah, covenant, sacrifice, resurrection, God's Word, and so forth to those who know only pagan gods? Early missionaries would have had to be knowledgeable not only of the Gentile world, but also of the world of Judaism. Paul's training as a Pharisee makes him an ideal candidate for this task of translation. His letters point to an early life deeply engaged in Scripture and theology. Because of this theological education, Paul was able to explain clearly to Gentiles both how Jesus Christ is the fulfillment of God's promises to the Jews and how this salvation has now been extended to them.

A Not-So-Obvious Choice

But the truly amazing thing for most of us is how the most defining characteristic of the early Paul makes him the last person we would expect God to choose. Paul persecuted the church. He imprisoned Christians, an act that sometimes led to their death (Acts 22:4; Gal. 1:13). Paul hated Jesus Christ and what he considered to be the blasphemy he brought. Is there any other biblical personality who needs to be so radically changed before he can serve? We know that God often calls unlikely people: Moses lacks speaking skills; David is young and impulsive; Peter is a Galilean without poise and education. But for Paul, this unlikely call involves not just empowerment for ministry, but also a total transformation of his essential beliefs. Of course, we affirm that Paul worships the God of Israel before and after his conversion. But before he sees the light on the road to Damascus, Paul "defines" God in a way that intentionally excludes Jesus Christ. To us, the early Paul is an incredibly unlikely choice for ministry because he actually believes that persecution of Christ and the church is an act of faithfulness to God.

Paul, Alienated from God

Foremost of Sinners

How could Paul have been so self-deluded? Neither Acts nor Paul's own letters spend much time discussing Paul's relationship with God before he came to know Christ. The few passages that do speak of this issue depict the early Paul as a prime example of human sinfulness. Because Paul persecuted the church, he describes himself as "the least of the apostles, unfit to be called an apostle" (1 Cor. 15:9). Paul acknowledges that before Christ confronted him on the road to

Damascus, he knew him (Christ) "from a human point of view," a common way of describing a worldly or sinful attitude (2 Cor. 5:16). Although it was most certainly written by a follower of Paul rather than by Paul himself, I think that 1 Timothy 1:15–17 sums up the apostle's pre-Christ identity very well:

> The saying is sure and worthy of full acceptance, that Jesus Christ came into the world to save sinners—of whom I am the foremost. But for that very reason I received mercy, so that in me, as the foremost, Jesus Christ might display the utmost patience, making me an example to those who would come to believe in him for eternal life.

Paul is the archetype of sinners: if he can be saved, anybody can be saved! Although these words stress Paul's "achievement" in sinning, something that does not surprise us, what is also communicated is how Paul's sin is like our sin and how the salvation he receives is like what we are all given. When Paul talks about sin in his letters, he is speaking from experience and in a way that links him to all humanity.

Paul is certainly aware of individual sins and the problems they cause.[2] But more important than these acts of disobedience is *Sin,* a term that for Paul describes our rebellion against God. Beginning with Adam, history is the story of Sin and salvation, humans fleeing from God, and God seeking to reestablish a relationship with them, culminating in the mission of Christ (Rom. 5:12–17). Perhaps the best evidence for this relational definition of Sin in Paul comes in the terms he uses to describe what God brings us in Jesus Christ. To those who have separated themselves from God, God offers reconciliation, justification, adoption, and love, to name a few blessings.[3] For Paul, God is a seeking God, one who desires a relationship with us even though we, whether through ignorance or arrogance, often try to flee from God.

Arrogant Disobedience

Romans 1:18–3:20 is Paul's clearest statement about our disobedience to God. Both Gentiles and Jews rebel against God's standards for worship and human behavior. Gentiles, even apart from Scripture, know about God's "eternal power and divine nature" through the world around them (1:20). But they choose to abandon God, and they dishonor him by creating idols to suit their own needs (1:21–23). Jews, according to Paul, are no less arrogant. Even though they have all the advantages that come with being God's chosen people (2:17–20), they intentionally disobey God (2:21–24). Above all, Paul wants to show how breaking God's natural or revealed law discloses our attitude toward God. Look carefully at the list in Romans 1:28–32. In their wickedness, evil, covetousness, malice, and so forth, Gentiles show themselves to be essentially "God-haters" (1:29–30). And the hypocrisy of Jews leads to the blasphemy of God (2:24). It's no wonder that Paul can later describe those whom Christ came to save as "enemies" of God (Rom. 5:10). Even though he never explicitly talks about himself in terms of this arrogant disobedience, his closing statement about who sins in this way ("all, both Jews and Greeks"; 3:9) surely means that he includes himself in this category as well.

Ignorant Obedience

Paul does, however, speak about Sin in his preconversion life as a kind of ignorant obedience. Philippians 3:2–11 is a fascinating passage. There Paul lists his Jewish credentials as a mock defense of himself against the Jewish Christians who are bothering the church at Philippi. What a remarkable vita! His pedigree and achievements are impeccable: circumcised, located within the covenant community, trained as a Pharisee, a zealous persecutor of the church, and *blameless under the law* (3:5–6). This is not a portrait of a weak or rebellious man, but one who is doing everything he can to please God! And yet there is something flawed about this obedience. Paul goes on to say that he came to consider all of these "good" things as "loss" or even "rubbish" after Jesus Christ became his Lord (3:7–8). Translators have here succumbed to the desire to make the text palatable for a wide audience: "rubbish" would be far better translated with our slang word for excrement! In the strongest possible terms, Paul is saying that even the best he has to offer does not put him right with God.

I think we can rightly claim this too as a kind of Sin in Paul, a way that we become separated from God. How does an attempt to obey God lead *away* from God? I wish Paul had said more about this, although there are some clues. Note in 3:9 how he contrasts righteousness that comes from faith in Christ with "a righteousness of my own." Did Paul pursue obedience to God in a way that emphasized *his* role in the quest or perhaps made his religion into a set of tasks to be completed rather than a living relationship with the divine? A similar note is sounded in Romans 10:2–3 as Paul speaks of his fellow Jews:

> I can testify that they have a zeal for God, but it is not enlightened. For, being ignorantof the righteousness that comes from God, and *seeking to establish their own*, they have not submitted to God's righteousness. (emphasis added)

What is it about humans that makes us distort even good tasks into declarations of independence from God? How can we be so ignorant about the kind of righteousness God desires?

Romans 7:7–25 is an important passage for this topic as well. The "I" Paul uses here is rhetorical: he is speaking about all of humanity in relationship to the law. Still, I think that Paul himself has experienced the inner turmoil he is describing. Perhaps we could say that these verses express the middle ground between arrogant disobedience and ignorant obedience. Paul, like all of us, can will what is right, but he "cannot do it" (7:18). Here Paul is not defending himself, and we see none of the confidence about keeping the law found in Philippians 3:6. We immediately relate to the dilemma that Paul describes. We can't make ourselves righteous before God, no matter how hard we try. Sin always wins out (7:23). Paul emphasizes the power of Sin by personifying it and describing it as another law (7:19–20, 23). Humans have a glimpse of what God wants, perhaps even a desire for it (7:22), but we are enslaved by Sin (7:23; 6:15–19). I have no doubt that when Paul writes "Wretched man that I am" (7:24), he is expressing what he himself has felt.

An Evil World

Paul's personification of sin or evil in Romans 7:19–20 (above) is one of many places where he intimates that our alienation from God results from more than just human rebellion. Like many Jews of his day, Paul believes that the world is the scene of a cosmic war between

God and Satan. An evil power exists that seeks to lead us away from God. In 2 Corinthians 4:4 he actually calls it "the god of this world." In Ephesians 2:2 it is labeled "the ruler of the power of the air." Most often he refers to Satan's kingdom with the term "elemental spirits" (see Gal. 4:3, 9; Col. 2:8, 20). This understanding of cosmic evil that is hostile to God is typical of Jewish apocalypticism, a movement I will discuss early in the next chapter. For our purposes here, what is important is how Paul's view of Satan emphasizes even more humanity's susceptibility to Sin. Like all humans apart from Christ, the early Paul is enslaved to things that make a relationship with God impossible, whether that slavery is seen primarily in terms of his own inability to be righteous before God, or whether it is viewed as a product of God's enemy, Satan (Rom. 6:19).

Paul for Today

Is there a more chilling statement about Paul than the one we find in Acts 8:1: "And Paul approved of their killing him [Stephen]"? It lies at the heart of what the New Testament witnesses about the early Paul. *Paul persecuted the church and opposed the gospel of Jesus Christ.* Looking back, it is obvious that Paul was engaged in the same kind of self-deception about God that so often characterizes "religion." His Sin, whether it is seen primarily as ignorance or arrogance, looks very much like our own. Paul's own claim that he was "set apart before [he] was born" (Gal. 1:15) makes us wonder how God was shaping him in these early years, and there is much in Paul's training and experience that God would use when he became a Christian missionary. But it is especially the inappropriateness of him as a candidate to be a leader in the early church that makes us stand in awe of God's wonderful plan of salvation.

Whenever I teach about Paul in the church, people want to discuss the early Paul, the Paul who is ignorant of true righteousness and who is enslaved to his own religious zeal. Christians want to talk about various kinds of alienation from God because they have experienced them so powerfully, before, and even to some extent after, they came to know Christ. Paul epitomizes the human predicament. We see ourselves in him. How could we be so ignorant as to rebel against God or hate God? How could we be so foolish as to think that God fails to discern our self-serving motives in religion? Paul reminds us of our Sin, but does so in a way that also reminds us of the lengths to which God will go to redeem us from that Sin. As we shall see in the next chapter, even Paul is changed. Only when we grasp how little the early Paul resembles the man he would become can we begin to see the magnitude of Christ's revelation to him on the road to Damascus.

Questions for Discussion

1. Which kind of Sin has been most prevalent in your life: arrogant disobedience or ignorant obedience?
2. In light of the fact that Paul follows the same God before and after his experience on the road to Damascus, is it legitimate to call it a conversion?
3. What is the relationship between law and obedience? Does having a law in place motivate you to keep it, or is some other motivation necessary?

Paul's Conversion and Call

Biblical Texts: Acts 9:1–22; 22:4–16; 26:9–18; Galatians 1:11–17

"The Fullness of Time"

It is impossible to understand the actions and teachings of Paul without a grasp of his apocalyptic worldview. Apocalypticism (based on a Greek word meaning "revelation") is not a religion in and of itself, but a way of thinking about religion and society.[1] There are two major themes in Jewish apocalypticism that directly influence Paul's thought. First of all, apocalypticism affirms that the world is largely under the control of Satan and that history is doomed. Often the severity of the trauma experienced by humans, especially God's chosen people, indicates the closeness of the end. When Paul speaks of "the present evil age" (Gal. 1:4), when he says that "the present form of this world is passing away" (1 Cor. 7:31), or speaks of the "elemental spirits" (Col. 2:8, 20; etc.; see chap. 2), we see how much he has been influenced by this type of thinking. Second, apocalypticism believes that in the near future God's rule will replace the current evil world. There will be an "apocalypse," a revelation, or disclosure of the new age. It will be ushered in by a messianic figure, often referred to as the "Son of Man" (see Daniel and *1 Enoch*). The new age will arrive as an unmistakable event: planetary bodies will fall, people will be raised from the dead, and all of life will be renewed under God's rule.

It is obvious that Paul not only accepts the idea of a new age; he also believes the new age *has arrived* in Jesus Christ. "Christ has been raised," a sure sign of the presence of God's kingdom (1 Cor. 15:20). And human beings who live in Christ can now be called "a new creation" (2 Cor. 5:17). We experience God's love in a profoundly new way. But notice how this affirmation of the presence of the new age in Jesus Christ challenges the typical Jewish apocalyptic timeline. In Paul's thought (like that of Jesus in the Gospels) we find no neat distinction between old age and new age. Sin and satanic rule continue, even after Christ has arrived. No cosmic signs have been observed: the sun, moon, and stars continue to follow their heavenly paths. Although Jesus "has been raised from the dead, the first fruits" of what will be (1 Cor. 15:20–28), yet in the present, humans both die and remain unraised. For Paul, the old age and the new age overlap. An awareness of this tension between what we already experience in Jesus Christ and what we do not yet experience of God's rule is absolutely essential to an understanding of Paul's life as a Christian.

One could certainly begin the story of Paul's new life with the extraordinary events that occurred on the road to Damascus. But when Paul tells the story, he always puts it in the context of God's larger purposes. What happened to Paul that day is one manifestation of the pivotal event that happened some four or five years earlier. Christ's death and resurrection mark the *apocalypsis,* or revelation, of the new age. All of creation had been longing for the freedom and glory that the messiah would bring (Rom. 8:18–25). Christ arrived according to God's purposes in "the fullness of time" (Gal. 4:4). Paul makes it clear that Christ's resurrection signals a larger drama of salvation, of which his experience on the road to Damascus is only one small part.

Paul's Revelation

Confronted by the Living Christ

Acts tells the full story three times (Acts 9:1–22; 22:1–16; 26:9–23), and Paul refers to it in several of his letters (see esp. 1 Cor. 9:1; 15:3–11; Gal. 1:13–17). In my opinion, no other incident recorded in the

Bible more clearly illustrates God's power to change people. Not long after he participated in the stoning of Stephen, while he was on the way to Damascus to persecute Jewish Christians there (perhaps about the year 34 or 35), the risen Christ appeared to Paul. Acts describes it as a concrete historical event perceptible to those traveling with Paul and not simply a personal vision (9:7; 22:9). Christ appears to Paul in a bright light that blinds him and knocks him to the ground. And Christ confronts him with the words that go to the heart of his delusional religious zeal; "Saul, Saul, why do you persecute me?" (9:4; 22:7; 26:14). As if this indictment were not enough to identify his heavenly visitor, Paul meekly asks him who he is. Christ states clearly that he is Jesus, the very person Paul is persecuting (9:5; 22:8; 26:15). He then tells the humbled and blind Paul to go into Damascus to await further instructions. There the disciple Ananias, instructed by a vision from the Lord, restores Paul's sight, baptizes him in the name of Jesus Christ, and tells Paul about his call to proclaim the good news, especially to the Gentiles (9:15; 22:15, 21; 26:17).

Paul's words about the event in his letters are much briefer but make it no less pivotal. The account in Galatians occurs in the context of a defense of Paul's apostleship (Gal. 1:10–17). Paul doesn't repeat the indicting words of Jesus found in Acts ("Saul, Saul, why do you persecute me?"), but he does emphasize his former life as a persecutor of the church (Gal. 1:13–14) as a way of showing how radically he has been changed through this encounter with Christ. He has come to know that the one whom he had been persecuting is in fact *God's Son* (1:16)! Above all, Paul wants to convey the nature and power of his call. What he received that day on the road to Damascus was a *revelation* from God (an *apocalypsis*: 1:12, 16; cf. 2:2), a glimpse of the new age that comes in Jesus Christ and his resurrection. This revelation of Christ transforms, to be sure, but it also gives a mission to the one who is transformed. Christ reveals to Paul that he has been set apart for God's work (1:15) and that his specific task is the proclamation of the good news to the Gentiles (1:16; see also 2:2, 8–10). Paul sees the risen Christ (1 Cor. 9:1) in what he considers to be the last of the resurrection appearances (1 Cor. 15:5–8). He is radically changed. Paul is given a call that is the polar opposite of his former work.

Paul's Conversion

Biblical scholars often debate whether Paul's experience was a conversion or a call.[2] As the term is used with respect to religion, "conversion" is usually defined as the change people experience when they move from a life lived apart from God to a life lived in relationship to God. Was Paul converted that day on the road to Damascus? On the one hand, there are ways that Paul's experience does not fit the traditional definition. Paul is devoted to the same God before and after this revelation. Over and over in his letters, he makes it clear that Jesus Christ is the fullest revelation of the God of Israel, the God who justified Abraham by faith and gave his people the law (Rom. 4–7; Gal. 3; et al.). Paul's whole life has been governed by an attempt to be righteous before God (Phil. 3:4–6). He certainly does not bring to mind a convert at a revival meeting or a mission church!

On the other hand, Paul does experience a radical change in his definition of God and how he should relate to God. Yes, Paul serves the same God after his revelation of Christ, but God is now defined as the God who sends his Son, Jesus Christ. And Paul's relationship with God is now based on grace and love and freedom rather than the constraints of the law. Even with his carefully groomed religious facade, the pre-Christ Paul is no less a sinner standing in need of forgiveness than the rest of us. Just as important, Paul's task as a disciple is radically altered because of his revelation. In his former life he condemned those who serve Christ; now he himself stands ready to suffer and die for Christ. Both Acts and Paul's Letters stress the almost incomprehensible gulf between the former and latter Paul by contrasting the words "persecutor" and "proclaimer": "The one who formerly was persecuting us is now proclaiming the faith he once tried to destroy" (Gal. 1:23).

Paul's Call

All of the accounts of Paul's encounter with Christ on the road to Damascus emphasize that he is being called to a specific task: proclaiming the gospel to the Gentiles. Each of the stories in Acts depicts Paul's reception of this commission in slightly different ways. In Acts

9:15 Ananias, the Christian at Damascus who is used to restore Paul's sight, is told by the Lord that "he [Paul] is an instrument whom I have chosen to bring my name before Gentiles." In Acts 22:12–21 Ananias tells Paul that he will be a "witness to all the world" (v. 15), but the specifics of that mission come directly to a Paul fearful of retaliation at the hands of Jewish Christians: "Go, for I will send you far away to the Gentiles" (v. 21). The fullest account of this commission, found in Acts 26, also comes directly to Paul and at the time of his revelation. After blinding him in a heavenly light (v. 13), the risen Jesus tells Paul that he is being sent to the Gentiles, "to open their eyes so that they may turn from darkness to light" (v. 18). What a powerful way of linking Paul's own blindness and new sight with his task of bringing light to the Gentiles!

Paul's own account in Galatians stresses his call more than his conversion (1:11–17). The most remarkable thing about Paul's words is his assertion that God had been grooming him for outreach to the Gentiles since before he was born (v. 15)! The language is very similar to call stories found in the prophets. God tells Jeremiah:

> Before I had formed you in the womb I knew you;
> and before you were born I consecrated you;
> I appointed you a prophet to the nations.
> (Jer. 1:4–5)

And Isaiah asserts,

> The LORD [Yahweh] called me before I was born,
>   while I was still in my mother's womb he named me.
> . . . .
> And now [Yahweh] says,
>   who formed me in the womb to be his servant,
> . . . .
> "I will give you as a light to the nations,
>   that my salvation may reach to the end of the earth."
> (Isa. 49:1–6)

Paul counters those in the churches of Galatia who think he lacks authority for his ministry by affirming that he has experienced a life-changing revelation from Christ, a call that was part of God's plan from the very beginning. To recognize Paul's call in that event actually makes his conversion all the more radical. Paul, the "foremost" of "sinners" (1 Tim. 1:15–16), a "blasphemer, a persecutor, and a man of violence" (v. 13), not only becomes a recipient of Christ's love and mercy (vv. 13–14); he actually also becomes an emissary of Christ! Paul's call is not something apart from his conversion; rather, it is proof of how fully God changes him.

Paul for Today

A Seeking God

Paul's conversion/call is a wonderful real-life example of a theme Jesus illustrates so well in his parable of the Prodigal Son (Luke 15:11–32). No matter what the younger son has done, the father, the character representing God in this parable, seeks to welcome him back (15:20–24). He is even patient with the self-righteous older son (vv. 25–32), an aspect of the story that also presents interesting parallels to that of Paul. In our last chapter we saw the extent of Paul's alienation from God. He hates Jesus Christ and tries to kill those who worship him. He deludes himself into thinking that he can please God simply by keeping the law. But even Paul's religious zeal *against* God cannot sabotage God's plan for his life. Here lies the most important thing to be learned from Paul's life, a theme mentioned in our opening chapter and one that we will return to over and over again: *In Jesus Christ, God seeks to reestablish a relationship with human beings.*

Later we will discuss other ways Paul speaks about how Christ saves us, especially the term "justification." But for now it is enough to recognize that one of the key terms Paul uses to describe what happens when Christ comes in to our lives is "reconciliation" (Rom. 5:6–11; 2 Cor. 5:18–20). According to Paul, it is always *we* who need to be reconciled to God. We have alienated ourselves from him. God is the one who initiates a new relationship, one that marks the beginning of the new age. Can we in the church again hear the power and joy of this message? It's difficult, I'm afraid, because this message of salvation is simultaneously radical and common. It is common in that we have heard the message time and time again, often in diluted or overly theological forms, and we have become hardened to it. It has become like the John 3:16 banners waving in the end zone, more of a nuisance or embarrassment than good news. In part it has become common *because* it is so radical. Can we begin to comprehend the message of Paul's revelation, that the God of the universe, the maker and sustainer of all things, seeks to have a loving relationship with us? Often it is easier to ignore it than to hear it.

The New Paul

How was Paul's life changed that day on the road to Damascus? *Everything* was changed, to the extent that one wonders how he survived the shock of it all. Friends became enemies, and enemies became beloved brothers and sisters in Christ. Paul's old job was gone, and he suddenly found himself with a new task, this one assigned by God! Many of his core religious beliefs were now suspect. If this Jesus was the Messiah, this man who had given himself on a cross to bring salvation to all people, then surely Paul had to rethink the place of law and temple as a path to righteousness. And if Jesus Christ was alive, raised from the dead, then the new age had already been inaugurated! Everything was given a new urgency. Most of all, Paul found himself in a new relationship with God that he could never have anticipated. God "grabbed" him and changed him and freed him. God's plan for salvation, his love for the world, is so strong that even a zealous persecutor of the church can be converted into a missionary for the gospel. Perhaps for the first time, Paul felt God's irresistible claim upon his life. And it was precisely in this vulnerability before God that Paul experienced the joy and peace of God's empowering grace (2 Cor. 12:9–10).

Can you relate to this transformational experience of Paul? Do you remember a time when the good news of Jesus Christ took hold of you and filled you with both joy and a new sense of urgency for living the Christian life? If we can grasp what Paul experienced when he was confronted by the risen Christ, we can also begin to understand Paul as person and missionary. What at first might appear to be authoritarian (1 Cor. 4:14–21) or boastful (2 Cor. 11–12) or dogmatic (Gal. 1:6–9) is, in reality, the expression of one who is absolutely convinced of the truth of the gospel and his call to lead others to Christ. No other single factor accounts for the passion of Paul more than the revelation he experienced on his way to persecute Christians.

Questions for Discussion

1. Do you have an experience of transformation in Christ that you can share with the class? How has it defined your life?
2. Name particular events in Paul's ministry or words in his letters that are explained in part by his Damascus road experience.
3. Does conversion always come with a call, as it does in Paul's case? How have you experienced God's call?

4

Paul's Early Steps as a Missionary

Biblical Texts: Acts 9:10–12:25; Galatians 1:17–24

Preliminaries

Three Journeys?

Students of Acts often refer to Paul's three missionary journeys (see 13:1–14:28; 15:36–18:22; 18:23–20:38). However, the author of Acts does not number these journeys, nor does he always make it clear where one ends and another begins. It is likely that he does not see them as three distinct journeys, but rather as several journeys separated by prolonged stays in certain churches, as was the case in Corinth or Ephesus (18:11; 20:31). In his letters, Paul himself never states or even implies that he was on only three missionary journeys. In fact, there is almost no information in Paul's Letters about the so-called first missionary journey, even though Acts dedicates two chapters to this journey into parts of Cyprus and Asia Minor (chaps. 13–14). In spite of these historical questions about the number of missionary journeys Paul took, there is wisdom, I think, in retaining this method of dividing Paul's travels. In a sometimes-bewildering series of cities, seas, continents, and ethnic groups, thinking in terms of three trips is a helpful learning device, and I will be using it in this book. I might also add that following the apostle's progress on one of the maps in the back of your Bible is vital to understanding the scope of his travels.

Paul or Acts: Do They Agree?

In this chapter we will begin to see some of the tensions between Paul's account of his missionary career and that found in Acts. One obvious example has to do with Paul's relationship with the Jerusalem church: did he go there soon after his conversion, meeting with all the apostles (Acts 9:26–27), or did he, as Paul himself says, go to Jerusalem later, "after three years" (Gal. 1:18), and then meet only with Peter and James (vv. 18–19)? This is a significant discrepancy, and the first of many. Another tension between Paul and Acts, especially concerning this early part of Paul's missionary career, is the fact that Acts records so much information about events that Paul never even mentions (i.e., 9:26–30; 11:19–30; 12:24–25). Where did the author of Acts get his information, and is it correct? Although it will be impossible to resolve these historical issues, I will begin to illustrate how differences concerning the writers' setting and motivation make these tensions less of an issue for Christians.

Paul in Acts before His "First" Journey

Changed and Empowered

The Acts account of Paul's activities after his call/conversion and before his first journey (chaps. 13–14) occurs in 9:10–30; 11:19–30; and 12:24–25. These episodes are intentionally interspersed with stories about Peter, Cornelius, and outreach to Gentiles (9:32–11:18) and King Herod's persecution of the church (12:1–23). After meeting the risen Christ, the blinded Paul goes to Damascus (9:8). God sends Ananias to him (9:10–16), and he is enabled by God to restore Paul's sight (9:12, 18). God's words to Ananias about Paul's mission are very telling. He is told both that Paul's mission will be especially to the Gentiles (9:15; exactly what Paul reports in Gal. 1:16) and that his mission will involve suffering (Acts 9:16). Paul's response to his encounter with Christ is the same as it is for other converts in Acts; he is baptized and is filled with the Holy Spirit (vv. 17–18).

Acts gives us almost no specifics about the duration of this early period, but it does tell us that by the time Paul began his so-called first missionary journey (13:1–3), he had already ministered in Damascus (9:19b–29), Tarsus (9:30; 11:25), and Antioch (11:26–27) and had made two trips to the church in Jerusalem (9:26–28; 11:27–30).

Certainly one of the key reasons for the author of Acts to write about this period of Paul's life is to show the extent to which he has been changed and empowered. The Paul who formerly condemned the Jews following Jesus now proclaims in synagogues that Jesus is the Son of God and Messiah (9:19b–22). Imagine the self-effacing boldness it took to argue with one's fellow Jews against the stance Paul himself took a few weeks earlier! Imagine how difficult it would have been to face the apostles and Christians in Jerusalem (9:26–28), let alone proclaim the gospel to them. It's no wonder, as Acts puts it, that people "were amazed" (9:21). This is clear confirmation that Paul's call has been effective and that the Holy Spirit is powerful indeed.

This section of Acts also emphasizes Paul's empowerment by showing his willingness to engage (and enrage!) his opponents. He so aggravates a group of Jews in Damascus that they plot to kill him (9:23–24). Paul is able to escape only by being let down in a basket through an opening in the wall (9:25; cf. 2 Cor. 11:32–33). Later, in Jerusalem, Paul argues with some Hellenists (in this case, Greek-speaking Jews) who also seek to kill him (9:29). Once again, believers help him escape (v. 30). The author of Acts is not only foreshadowing the conflict and suffering Paul would experience later; he is also giving confirmation to the second part of God's words concerning Paul to Ananias: "I myself will show him how much he must suffer for the sake of my name" (9:16). There is no greater proof of one's convictions than a willingness to suffer and even die for them.

Shaped and Led

We might have expected that after God's declaration that Paul would "bring my name before Gentiles" (Acts 9:15), Paul would immediately be involved in Gentile mission, especially since he himself emphasizes this aspect of his call (Gal. 1:16). But Acts gives no clear indication that Paul reaches out to Gentiles until 11:19–26. There we are told that those who are scattered to Phoenicia, Cyprus, and Antioch as a result of the persecution that arose after the stoning of Stephen

(8:1) initially preach only to Jews (11:19). This changes, however, when certain unnamed Christians from Cyprus and Cyrene proclaim the gospel to "Hellenists," in this instance meaning "Gentiles."[1] The success of this Gentile mission in Antioch comes to the attention of church leaders in Jerusalem, and Barnabas is sent to investigate (11:22). Barnabas approves of this successful outreach to Gentiles (11:23–24), and it is he who goes to Tarsus to bring Paul into this new ministry (11:25–26). We are told that the two work with the Gentiles in Antioch for a full year with great success, even to the extent that this new group of followers is given a name that distinguishes them from Jewish believers (11:26). They are now called "Christians."

Paul does become involved in Gentile mission (and will continue his outreach to Jews as well), but we need to note carefully what initiates that mission. Acts makes it very clear that Paul is *led* by God to his ministry in Antioch, in this case through the church, God's empowered emissary in the world, and its servant Barnabas. God has a plan by which the gospel of Jesus Christ will be spread throughout the world (1:8). Paul is not a "free agent" in Acts. Even in this time before his first mission, it is clear that he is being shaped and preserved by the church for God's purposes. Ananias is told very specifically by God what to say to Paul and what to do. Disciples in Damascus help him escape Jews trying to kill him (9:25). Paul consults the apostles in Jerusalem (9:26–27). Believers help him elude the Hellenists in Jerusalem (9:30). He is called by Barnabas to serve in the church at Antioch, then sent by this same church with aid to the church in Judea (11:25–30). That God is leading Paul, sometimes though guidance and contact with the church, at other times through direct revelation through the Holy Spirit (see 16:7–10), is one of the most important themes in Acts. Perhaps we are even justified in calling this early period of Paul's mission "preparatory." In his discussions with Jews in Damascus, Acts reports that Paul's words became "increasingly more powerful" (9:22). The early ministry experiences of Paul in Damascus, Tarsus, and Antioch, his debates with Jews, his experiences of danger, his developing relationship with the Jerusalem church, and certainly his yearlong Gentile ministry (11:26)—all of these are ways that Paul is made ready for the call of the Holy Spirit to his first missionary journey (13:2).

Paul before the "First" Journey according to the Letters

Unlike Acts, Paul in his letters says very little about either his ministry immediately after his conversion or what we are calling his "first missionary journey" (as found in Acts 13–14). As was so concerning his call/conversion, the key resource is Galatians. He does, however, give us a few tantalizing bits of information, most of which appear to be in conflict with what we read in Acts. Remember that Paul is writing the church at Galatia to reestablish his authority over against certain Jewish Christians who are trying to convince the Gentile Christians there that they must observe torah, or the Jewish law. One of his tactics is to show that his call is from God and is not based upon human authority (Gal. 1:12, 15–16). And so when he writes about his early years in ministry, he stresses his independence from the leaders of the Jerusalem church. In contrast to the details of ministry in Damascus and visit to the Jerusalem church as reported in Acts 9, Paul simply says that after his call "I did not confer with any human being, nor did I go up to Jerusalem to those who were already apostles before me" (Gal. 1:16b–17).

Where did Paul go? Paul says he went to Arabia and then returned to Damascus, spending a total of three years in those places (Gal. 1:17–18). In Paul's day Arabia referred to the Nabatean kingdom, the area to the south of Israel whose capital was Petra. What did he do there? Paul gives us one clue. In 2 Corinthians 11:32–33 Paul states that he had been pursued by King Aretas in Damascus earlier in his career, but that he was able to escape by being let down in a basket through a window in the wall. This same Aretas ruled both Damascus *and* the Nabatean kingdom in the late 30s CE. Is it possible that Aretas sought to arrest Paul in Damascus because of trouble he caused two or three years earlier in Nabatea?[2] This would mean that Paul did not go to Arabia for spiritual reflection or preparation, as some have suggested, but that he engaged in mission there to the extent that he upset the authorities. It is also fascinating to see that both Acts and Paul talk about a daring escape from Damascus early in the apostle's career, although the reasons given for hostility toward Paul are quite different (Acts 9:23–25; 2 Cor. 11:32).

Galatians says that Paul went to Jerusalem after three years in Arabia and Damascus. Although the Acts references to time can be ambiguous ("For several days," 9:19b; "After some time," 9:23; "When he had come," 9:26), it does appear to suggest that Paul went to Jerusalem soon after his conversion. This conflict, plus the fact that Paul asserts he saw only Peter and James during that visit (Gal. 1:18–22: "I was still unknown by sight to the churches of Judea"), while Acts declares that Paul met with all the apostles and the wider church in Jerusalem (Acts 9:26–28)—all make reconciliation of these accounts quite difficult.

Even though Paul chooses to say little about this period immediately after his confrontation by the risen Christ, the general outlines are clear. Paul relates his departure to Arabia, his time spent in Damascus, and his trip to meet the leaders of the Jerusalem church because they represent his faithful response to Jesus Christ. He does not return to his former life of persecuting the church. He does not need to "confer with any human being" (Gal. 1:16). He has been changed'and is secure in his call. It is most probable that Paul begins to proclaim the gospel soon after his conversion/call. In light of 2 Corinthians 11:32–33 (above), his trip to Arabia (Nabatea), a non-Jewish region, is best seen as his first attempt at Gentile mission. When Paul goes to Jerusalem some fourteen years later (Gal. 2:1), his primary concern is that what he has been doing, *proclaiming the gospel among the Gentiles*, might not somehow have been in vain (Gal. 2:2). This is Paul's essential characterization of his activity during this early period.

Paul for Today

What Really Happened?

Do the historical tensions between Acts and Paul's Letters concerning this early period in his ministry disturb you? If they do, then this is fair warning: we will continue to see these tensions in our study, some concerning events in Paul's life and others concerning the nature of his teachings. As modern human beings, we have come to assume that we should be able to discover *what really happened*. Moreover, it is often our assumption that the historical event is the only safe foundation on which truth can be built. Our reaction to a book placed on (and soon removed from) Oprah's reading list, *A Million Little Pieces*,[3] is a good example of this mind-set. I certainly agree that book publishers need to carefully distinguish between fiction and nonfiction, but I have often wondered what our quick dismissal of books *because they are not historically verifiable* might suggest about our attitude toward the Bible.

How can Christians respond to these historical issues? First of all, we need to be very clear about the different motivations Paul (in this case, re Galatians) and the author of Acts have for writing. In Galatians (written between 54 and 58 CE) we see a very high-pitched letter in which Paul is defending the church against certain Jewish Christians, perhaps best defined as the "circumcision faction" or the "people from James" (the brother of Jesus; 2:12). These outsiders have been trying to convince the Gentiles in Galatia that they must follow Jewish law in order to practice Christianity (1:9; 3:1–3; 4:17; 5:7–12; etc.). It is obvious that they are highly critical of Paul and his message of freedom from the law (1:10; 4:12–16; 5:1, 11–13; etc.). Paul writes the Galatians to show how wrong the teachings of these Jewish Christians are (from 2:15 to the end) and to defend himself and his authority as an apostle (1:10–2:14). In this first, biographical part of the letter, Paul's purpose is to show that his call and authority are from God and not from humans, and certainly not from the Jerusalem church, with which his opponents appear to be linked. In other words, the situation Paul is addressing in this later period of his ministry motivates him to downplay any human involvement immediately after his call, and especially involvement from the Jewish Christian church in Jerusalem.

Contrast this motivation with that of the writer of Acts. He writes some forty or so years after this early period in Paul's life that we have been discussing. Looking back upon events that took place some two generations earlier, he is motivated to write a history of the church that shows its faithfulness to God's leading in Jesus Christ, especially how it was led in a smooth transition from Jewish to Gentile Christianity. We see much less of the conflict between these groups in Acts that we see in Paul's Letters, and when the conflict is mentioned, as in Acts 11 and 15, the author tries to show how the church amicably solves its problems. In the part of Acts we have been studying, note how the author carefully balances sections about Paul with sections that deal with the Jerusalem church and its leadership (esp. Peter). After Paul's conversion and call to preach, especially to Gentiles (Acts 9:1–30), Peter and the Jerusalem church are given center stage (9:32–11:18); they too come to understand that the gospel is also for Gentiles (11:18). The fruit of this twofold recognition of the legitimacy of Gentile mission comes in 11:19–26 (see above), where *both* Barnabas (from the Jerusalem church) and Paul minister to Gentiles in Antioch. A joint mission by Paul and Barnabas to the poor in Judea (11:27–30; 12:25) brackets the next section about the Jerusalem church (12:1–24), which leads nicely to the first major missionary journey, again a joint venture by Barnabas and Paul (13:1–3). In Acts, God's leading of the Jerusalem church and God's leading of Paul are so interrelated that if the author had *not* spoken about Jerusalem's "approval" of the newly converted Paul, we would have been surprised (9:26–30)!

The way in which human motivations influence the writing of the biblical texts is a hard reality that cannot be avoided by Christians. Paul and the author of Acts write for quite different reasons and from quite different settings. What they say about Paul's life and teachings is not always reconcilable. It quickly becomes obvious that *people* wrote the Bible, people very much like us! And yet we affirm that out of these human words comes God's Word! This human involvement in the creation of Scripture raises an essential question: on what basis can we as Christians claim that the Bible is authoritative? The church has given three basic answers over the years. First of all, we say that God worked in the biblical writers, inspiring them to write the texts we now have (see 2 Tim. 3:16). This does not eliminate the human factor, but it does ensure that God stands behind the message of salvation we hear in Scripture. Second, we affirm that God was present in the church's selection of authoritative books, or the canonization process. The church, the body of Christ (1 Cor. 12:27; Eph. 4:1–16), under the guidance of the Holy Spirit, made the right choices about which books are worthy of being called God's Word. Third, Christians say that the Bible is authoritative because God reveals his truth to us in its reading and proclamation. As John Calvin puts it, Scripture is "self-authenticated" through the Holy Spirit.[4]

How do you react to these three ways of thinking about biblical authority? Notice what the three do *not* affirm: they do not say that the

Bible is authoritative because it is historically verifiable. Even though we may have a strong and legitimate urge to find out what "really happened," these traditional ways of thinking about biblical authority caution us not to make that the only factor in determining the truthfulness of Scripture. First-century writers did not have the "scientific" view of history that we often claim. Even when they disagree, Acts and Paul's Letters convey important truths about salvation in Jesus Christ that we must not ignore. We don't have to dismiss either Paul or Acts because they appear not to agree historically. Both Acts and Paul's Letters are God's word to us. They are two different yet two inspired accounts of what this early period in Paul's ministry means to us.

A God Who Acts

Even though Paul's Letters and Acts may disagree about the nature of Paul's contact with Jewish Christians in Jerusalem, they are very much in agreement on an important theme noted in our first chapter: *God is a God who acts in history for the salvation of his people.* In Galatians, the letter with which we have been dealing most, Paul's focus is upon God's actions *in him*, although in other Pauline Letters we will certainly see this broadened out to include God's actions in the church and in the world. God comes to Paul in revelations (Gal. 1:12, 16; 2:2; 1 Cor. 15:8) and visions (2 Cor. 12:1–4), and he receives confirmation of these revelations through the church (Gal. 2:1–12). Looking back upon this early period, Paul is obviously convinced that God was leading him to minister in Arabia and Damascus and to later visit Jerusalem. For the purpose of salvation of the Gentiles, God acts and Paul reacts.

Acts (9–12) emphasizes this same theme, but it is especially careful to show God acting *in the church*. God empowers both Paul and Peter, both the Antiochene church and the Jerusalem church, for a joint venture that will bring the gospel to the Gentiles. I know of no other place in the New Testament that speaks more powerfully about God's orchestration of events to achieve certain ends. In chapter 3 I spoke about God as a seeking God, but it is clear in Paul and Acts that God does more than just desire a relationship with humans. God also acts, and acts in powerful and premeditated ways to break down the barriers that have separated us from him. Here is the almost incomprehensible truth: God shapes history out of his love for us.

Theologians and philosophers like to describe our age as "postmodern." During the "modern" era (perhaps through the 1950s), there was some consensus about the presuppositions or "story" that shapes us: human industry, especially through science, is leading us to a better world. People could agree on the meaning of truth. But in our postmodern era, this consensus has disappeared. I see little agreement in our world on things that used to be assumed, especially concerning human dignity and the value of human life. According to postmodernists, all truth is local or individual.

I think it is extremely difficult for us as Christians, whether we see ourselves in a modern or postmodern environment, to have an assurance that God is acting in our world. Where do you see God shaping people and events in your everyday life? Do you have a sense of God's leading? Can you affirm that God is an active God, not just in your life but also in terms of a larger plan of salvation? The story of Paul reminds us in a powerful way that God is always working in the world to lead people to reconciliation. Recognizing God's hand in our world is one of the most countercultural things we do as Christians.

Questions for Discussion

1. How do you understand biblical authority? Give examples of how our modern view of history can be a problem for us when we read the Bible.
2. Think of ways in which your worship and practice of the faith acknowledge that God is working in our world. Give examples of times when you thought that God was absent.
3. It is also important to understand that God works in and through the church. Can you think of ways that your church shows God's plan for salvation?

5

The First Missionary Journey

Biblical Texts: Acts 13–14; 1 Corinthians 9:19–23; Romans 15:14–21

Filling the Gaps

The Letters of Paul say almost nothing about the period in his life that is given some attention in Acts 13–14, the time of his so-called first missionary journey. This is the period after the first trip to Jerusalem, which Paul records in Galatians 1:18 (three years after his conversion, roughly 39 CE), and before the Jerusalem council, a meeting that Paul says took place "after fourteen years" (again, counting from his conversion, i.e., 49 or 50 CE; Gal. 2:1). Concerning this approximately ten-year period, Paul says only that he "went into the regions of Syria and Cilicia" (Gal. 1:21). Paul's comment about why he made his second trip to Jerusalem, as a test of the legitimacy of his Gentile mission (2:2), most probably indicates that he was especially involved in Gentile ministry at this time. And his reference to a stoning in 2 Corinthians 11:25 might refer to the stoning at Lystra mentioned in Acts 14:19. Based upon Paul's Letters alone, however, we would have very few details about this segment of his ministry.

The Acts concern for this period in Paul's life centers upon a missionary trip he took with Barnabas, starting with his commissioning at the church at Antioch (Acts 13:2–3) and ending again at that church (14:26). In terms of distance covered, this is by far the shortest of Paul's missionary journeys. The writer of Acts give no indication of how much time was spent in these cities in Cyprus and Asia Minor, but if his visits were similar in length to those on his second and third journeys, then this entire first journey probably took no more than two years. That leaves at least eight years about which we have no information. Acts does assume that Paul continued in Gentile mission, however, because it clearly states that Paul (along with Barnabas) was sent to the Jerusalem council by the church at Antioch to argue for the full inclusion of Gentiles apart from circumcision (Acts 15:1–5).

Paul, the Mature Missionary

Sent by the Holy Spirit

Read Acts 13 and 14 carefully: they introduce several characteristics of what can be called the "mature" Paul, the articulate and empowered Paul we will see throughout the rest of Acts. The so-called first missionary journey of Paul focuses especially on three episodes, the confrontation of the magician Bar-Jesus in Paphos (13:6–12), Paul's sermon at Antioch in Pisidia (13:14–52), and the healing miracle at Lystra (14:8–18).

The writer of Acts obviously wants to distinguish this missionary work from what Paul has done previously. Important prophets and teachers are gathered at the church in Antioch: Barnabas, Simeon, Lucius, Manaen, and Paul (13:1). While they are worshiping and fasting, an indication that they are receptive to God's word, the Holy Spirit commands: "Set apart for me Barnabas and Saul [Paul] for the work to which I have called them" (13:2). After more fasting and praying, the group commissions them by the laying on of hands (13:3). Paul is being empowered by the Spirit in a way that sets this task apart. The Holy Spirit reveals his plan to a church body, and the body confirms it. What a wonderful example this is of the "external confirmation" of a call that we often speak about in the modern church, the way in which God's call to an individual is confirmed and supported by the Christian community!

In Acts, the Holy Spirit is especially that part of the Trinity that guides and empowers mission. Jesus predicts that when the Holy

Spirit comes upon them, the disciples will go to the ends of the earth with the gospel (Acts 1:8). And the Spirit empowers this mandate. Perhaps the most well-known example is that of Pentecost: after the disciples receive the Holy Spirit, they are given the ability to speak in other languages, and three thousand people are converted (2:1–4, 41). What we see concerning Paul in Acts 13 is very similar to the ways in which Peter is empowered according to Acts 2–3 immediately after his reception of the Spirit. Paul is given the ability to speak boldly and powerfully (cf. Peter and the disciples in 4:29–31). In Paphos, he sternly condemns the magician Bar-Jesus in front of the proconsul Sergius Paulus (13:9–10). In Antioch in Pisidia, Paul delivers a long and articulate sermon in the synagogue, the first of many recorded in Acts (13:16–41). In Lystra, when the locals think he is a god, Paul is able to give a response that is very much geared to his Gentile audience (14:15–17). Even though Paul calls himself "untrained in speech" (2 Cor. 11:6) and is wary of rhetoric as an end in itself (see 1 Cor. 1:17–2:5), his letters certainly confirm this gift of communication.

And there is a relationship between powerful word and deed. The author of Acts states that Paul and Barnabas stayed for a long time at Iconium, "speaking boldly for the Lord, who testified to the word of his grace by granting signs and wonders to be done through them" (14:3). Paul's Letters downplay his role as a miracle worker, but Acts immediately brings it to the fore as a "proof" of his empowerment through the Holy Spirit. In Acts 13:11 Paul blinds the magician Bar-Jesus through God's power, and as a result the proconsul believes (v. 12; cf. Peter and Simon the magician in 8:9–24). In 14:8–18 Paul heals a man who had been unable to walk since birth (v. 8; cf. Peter and the lame man in 3:1–10). Because of this great miracle, the Gentiles there count Barnabas as Zeus and Paul as Hermes, and Paul finds it very difficult to persuade them that they are only mortals (14:11–18). It is perhaps because of the potential for either the misunderstanding (here) or misuse of the power of the miracles (see 8:17–24 re Simon the magician) that we find them so seldom spoken of in Paul's Letters. When Paul does speak about his ability to perform miracles, he is very clear about the source of his power (Rom. 15:18–19). Paul is, as he says in 2 Corinthians, a "clay jar," a vessel used by God "so that it may be made clear that this extraordinary power belongs to God and does not come from us" (4:7).

Paul the Evangelist

Because Paul's voice comes to us primarily in his letters, it is wonderful to see Acts depict Paul as a preacher and actually give us a sampling of his sermons and speeches (in addition to the material in our section, see esp. 17:22–31; 21:27–22:29; 24:1–23; 25:23–26:32). Paul probably preached often, to both Jewish and Gentile audiences. According to Acts, Paul typically used the local synagogue as his starting point for mission in a new community (see 17:10; 18:4; etc.). Asking esteemed guests to make a comment on the Scripture read, as we see in 13:14–15, was not uncommon (compare Jesus' invitation to preach in his home synagogue in Luke 4:16–30).

It is probably best to see the lengthy sermon recorded in Acts 13:16–41 as the author's reconstruction of what Paul might have said based upon his sources and his knowledge of Paul. Scholars often note the similarity in terms of form and content between Paul's sermons and Peter's sermons in Acts, with the assumption that the author's hand shaped both. Still, there are several themes in the sermon that are quite consistent with what we read in his letters. Note the strong emphasis upon the roots of the story of Jesus in the old covenant (Acts 13:16–26) and his extensive interpretation of Scripture (13:33–41), elements common in Paul's Letters (Rom. 3–4, 9–11; 2 Cor. 3; Gal. 3–4; etc.). Notice also the sermon's concern with the rejection of Jesus by the Jews (cf. 1 Thess. 2:14–16; Romans 9:1–5; etc.). In this sermon there is a focus on the death and resurrection of Jesus (Acts 13:27–37), exactly what we find in the letters (1 Cor. 15:3–11; Gal. 3:10–14). And the words in Acts 13:39, that in Jesus we are justified by faith and not through the law of Moses, lie at the heart of Paul's message as we find it in the letters (Rom. 3–4; Galatians 2:15–21).

Paul may have been "untrained in speech" (2 Cor. 11:6), but his flourishing ministry indicates that he spoke very persuasively. Assuming that Acts 13:16–41 reflects what Paul said, or at least the kind of sermon typically used in the early church to evangelize Jews, what can we say about why it is effective? Why would his audience have listened when Paul preached this sermon? This sermon would have caught the attention of his hearers, first of all, because it speaks directly to the context of the audience. Almost everything in this sermon, from the initial "You Israelites" (v. 16) to the focused use of the Old Testament and the references to Abraham and David, calls out to the Jewish listener. More specifically, Paul is able to show his hearers how Jesus is the fulfillment of God's plan to bring forth a messiah through the people of Israel (13:16–26). How could they not listen? This is a personalized story of salvation, one that shows God responding to the longings of the ancestors of the very people listening. Paul knows his audience! In fact, this awareness of the deep spiritual needs of his hearers is one of the key reasons Paul was a successful missionary, although in his letters this insight is almost always directed toward a Gentile audience. As a good example of the latter in Acts, notice how effectively Paul switches gears when he addresses Gentiles in chapter 14 (vv. 15–18; cf. 17:22–31).

The second thing that makes this sermon effective, I think, is the clear focus on the death and resurrection of Jesus Christ (13:27–33). We know immediately what is central to the theology of the preacher. Jesus was killed, he was laid in a tomb, and he was raised by God from the dead (13:30, 33). Here we see no attempt to explain the function of the cross, although it is clear that it happens according to God's will (vv. 27–28). The resurrection is explained more fully: Jesus' resurrection indicates that he is the Son of God (13:33, quoting Ps. 2:7) and the firstfruits of the new age ("no more to return to corruption," v. 34; cf. 1 Cor. 15:20). I think we have to assume that Paul's Jewish audience would have understood a great deal about the meaning of cross ("tree"; see Gal. 3:13 and Deut. 21:23) and resurrection. Just as in Paul's Letters, the larger story of Jesus is not unimportant, but the urgency of this evangelistic sermon puts the spotlight on the salvific core of the message. A succinct retelling of the essential story has incredible power: a real human being died (for us) and was raised. Nothing like this has happened before! What could this mean?

The third thing that makes this sermon effective is the way Paul makes the human impact of the death and resurrection of Jesus ring out loud and clear. It is impossible to miss Paul's shift from the basic story of Jesus to the way in which it changes the lives of believers:

"Let it be known to you therefore" (Acts 13:38). And the content of this application is clear as well. Through the crucified and raised Jesus, there is forgiveness of sins (v. 38). Put differently (more typical of Paul), those who believe in Jesus are justified with God; they are freed from the burden of Sin in a way that the law of Moses could never achieve (v. 39). And as if this message were not enough to catch the attention of his hearers, Paul ends with a warning (vv. 40–41). "Beware," he says, quoting Habakkuk 1:5, that you do not become a scoffer who thinks this is all too wonderful to be true!

This is the bare bones of an effective sermon. It stands as a powerful example of effective evangelistic preaching because it tells the essentials of the salvation story in a way that is unavoidably relevant to the hearer; God wills it, Jesus fulfills it, and we are freed by it!

"To the Jew First and Also to the Greek"

The above phrase (Rom. 1:16) captures the essence of the New Testament's understanding of salvation history (God's plan for salvation for the world): the message of salvation is *to* the Jews and *through* the Jews to the entire world. Our passage in Acts illustrates so well how this "map" of salvation plays out in Paul's early ministry. His strategy is invariably to proclaim the message first in synagogues (Acts 13:5, 14), but he often receives strong opposition from the Jews (13:44–14:6). Note what he says to the Jews in Antioch in Pisidia after his conflict with them (13:46, 47):

> It was necessary that the word of God should be spoken first to you. Since you reject it and judge yourselves to be unworthy of eternal life, we are now turning to the Gentiles. For so the Lord has commanded us, saying,
>
> > "I have set you to be a light for the Gentiles,
> >   so that you may bring salvation to the ends of the earth."
> >   (quoting Isa. 49:6).

Readers might assume from this that Paul is giving up on mission to the Jews, but this is certainly not the case. The strategy of "Jew first and also to the Greek" continues in Acts in Paul's second and third journeys. But while Paul is effective in his ministry with many Jews, he continues to encounter hostility. Even the trouble that leads to his later arrest in Jerusalem and imprisonment in Rome comes at the hands of Jews from Asia (21:27). Acts concludes with words that echo the quote above. Speaking again to a group of Jews who are unable to accept his message, Paul says, "Let it be known to you then that this salvation of God has been sent to the Gentiles; they will listen" (28:28).

Two important questions grow out of this "Jew first, then Gentile" formula, ones with which Paul himself wrestled. The first is this: Why do the Jews not readily accept the message of salvation in Christ? Even though Paul knew that his call was primarily to Gentiles, this rejection by the Jews was a source of tremendous frustration for him (Rom. 9:1–5). The second is this: How is a message of salvation that has its origin in a Jewish context made understandable to Gentiles? This question obviously reflects theological concerns, but in Paul's case it is first and foremost a question about mission. Paul knew from the beginning that he had been called to Gentiles, but I am sure that he did not immediately grasp the complexity of his task of "translation."

Paul for Today

The story of Paul's life, whether it is drawn from Acts or Paul's own Letters, is all about mission. God calls Paul to evangelize, especially Gentiles. Paul is empowered by the Holy Spirit to effectively proclaim the good news. And God stands behind the progression of the gospel. As we shall see in a later chapter, even the failure of the Jews to accept Jesus Christ in the present is part of God's larger plan to reveal his mercy "to all" (Rom. 11:32). For Paul, being a Christian necessarily means participating in the advancement of God's kingdom.

To what extent should the mission of Paul be seen as a model for why and how we do mission in the contemporary church? I know well the arguments against this use of Paul: I have heard them often in class and even by missionaries. It is argued, first of all, that Paul's practice of mission cannot be easily applied to our world because the contexts are so different. Paul speaks to people who have never heard anything like the Christian message before. First-century hearers would not have been jaded by the half-truths, misinterpretations, and church divisions generated by two thousand years of Christian practice. Moreover, Paul's hearers would have been much more likely to feel the urgency of his message. Jesus' resurrection is the firstfruits of the general resurrection; he will soon come again to establish his kingdom (1 Cor. 15:20–28)! And context is important in terms of the plight of the common person in Paul's day. In a world where life was short, poverty and slavery were the norm, effective medicine did not exist, and much depended upon the goodwill of an arbitrary foreign government (Rome), think of the longing for a word of hope like that offered by the apostle!

In addition to these contextual differences, some argue that Paul is not normative for mission because he is so exceptional and gifted.[1] He experiences a unique and transforming call. He is incredibly bold and articulate in his proclamation of the gospel. He seems to have no fear in the face of danger and persecution (1 Cor. 15:30–32; 2 Cor. 11:22–12:10; Phil. 1:12–14; 4:10–13). Can we, as Paul does, conceive of ourselves as "ambassadors for Christ" (2 Cor. 5:20), people in whom the life of Christ is visible in all that we do (2 Cor. 4:11)?

How do you respond to these arguments? Is our world so different and Paul so unique that we have nothing to learn from his approach to evangelism? Certainly that is not the case. Yes, our worlds are different, and those engaged in outreach must always be highly aware of the context they are addressing. Paul himself is one of the best examples of the need for incarnational or contextual ministry ("to the Jews I became as a Jew . . . to the weak I became weak" (1 Cor. 9:20–22). But even though we may face challenges in mission that Paul did not have, I am convinced that in one essential way Paul's world and ours are alike: humanity still longs for some relief from its pain, loneliness, helplessness, and fear of death. Everywhere in Acts and Paul's Letters we see the apostle reaching out to people as if they have a desperate need for what he has to offer. Has that changed? The circumstances causing our despair may have changed, but the need for the message of hope in Christ has not. One of the most essential motivations for mission among Christians is the recognition that what people apart from Christ are missing is a life-and-death matter.

As to whether Paul represents an impossible missionary ideal, I think we need to hear the apostle's often-given invitation to see his changed life and vocation as an *example* (Phil. 3:17; 1 Tim. 1:16; "imitate me/us": 1 Cor. 4:16; 11:1; 1 Thess. 1:6; 2:14). Paul knows that different people are gifted in different ways (1 Cor. 12:4–11, 27–31), but his encouragement to believers to imitate him indicates that there are expressions of the new life in Christ that we all share: among them are love (1 Cor. 12:31–13:13), living in a way that is pleasing to God (Rom. 12), and, amazingly, becoming "the aroma of Christ to God among those who are being saved and among those who are perishing" (2 Cor. 2:15). In one of his strongest statements about mission, Paul says that all of us have been given "the ministry of reconciliation": we are "ambassadors for Christ" (2 Cor. 5:18–20). We cannot imitate Paul without grasping that his whole life is a response to God's reconciliation, a response that invariably includes a sharing of the gospel with others.

As David Bosch asks: How can we possibly take the apostle's life and writings seriously "unless we allow ourselves to be infected by the missionary passion of Paul?"[2] One of the key ways that Paul's life and writings speak to us, as we noted in the first chapter, is that they encourage us to come to terms with the link between our relationship with God in Christ and our task of spreading the good news: *As transformed people, we become witnesses to our salvation in Christ.*

Questions for Discussion

1. What kind of "translation" issues might we have when we speak to non-Christian Americans about Christ? In what ways might the Christian message sound odd or be challenging to them?
2. Besides Paul and other disciples in the New Testament, who are your Christian models? Whose life sets an example for how you live and how you express your faith?
3. Is there a difference between evangelism and mission? What do you think are the key reasons Paul was successful in his proclamation?

6

The Jerusalem Council

Biblical Texts: Galatians 2–4; Acts 15:1–35; Romans 3:21–8:39

After Fourteen Years

As we noted at the beginning of the last chapter, Paul states in Galatians 2:1 that after fourteen years in ministry, he made another trip to Jerusalem (ca. 49 or 50 CE). There he participated in what scholars often call the "Jerusalem council," an extremely important event both for Paul and for the early church. The council was a gathering of Christians that tried to define the extent to which Gentiles, an increasingly powerful segment of the church, should be required to obey Jewish law, including circumcision. Paul gives his account of the council in Galatians 2:1–14, and Acts addresses it in chapter 15. The differences between these two accounts present another good example of why finding the "historical Paul" is not always easy and why careful reading of the texts is so important.

The Council according to Acts

Representatives of Antioch

Antioch was deeply involved in Gentile mission. Through the invitation of Barnabas, Paul had come to Antioch to team with him to minister to the Gentiles there (Hellenists; Acts 11:20–26). As we have seen, the church at Antioch was also responsible for the commissioning of Paul and Barnabas on their first missionary journey together, one that was especially successful among Gentiles (13:46). This church was not only a pioneer in terms of openness to Gentiles; it also broke new ground in terms of what it demanded of Gentile Christians. When "certain individuals" came from Judea and were teaching that Gentile Christians must be circumcised according to the law (15:1), we are told that Paul and Barnabas "had no small dissension and debate with them" (15:2). Obviously the two, following the consensus at Antioch, did not demand circumcision for Gentile Christians. Paul and Barnabas are chosen by the church of Antioch to represent them in Jerusalem to discuss an already divisive issue: to what extent do Gentile Christians need to follow Jewish law (15:2)?

According to Acts, Paul and Barnabas's input at the meeting is fairly minimal. They are greeted warmly by the apostles and elders when they arrive (15:4), although their initial report about God's work among the Gentiles is critiqued by Christian Pharisees (15:5). At the meeting itself, Acts reports only that Paul and Barnabas share with the assembly "all the signs and wonders that God had done through them among the Gentiles" (15:12). It is Peter and James, the brother of Jesus, who play the major roles in the Acts version of the story.

The Church Unified

In Acts, the meeting begins with an eloquent speech by Peter about the inclusion of the Gentiles and how they too had received the Holy Spirit (15:7, 8; obviously a reference to Peter's vision about the clean and unclean and the conversion of Cornelius [10:1–11:18]). He argues that Gentiles, like Jews, are saved by grace through faith (15:9, 11), and that there is no reason to put upon them "a yoke" (full observance of the law) that Jews themselves have not been able to bear (15:10). James, the brother of Jesus, is apparently the designated leader, and he has the final say. He agrees that the message of salvation in Christ is for Gentiles as well (15:14–18). His decision is that Gentile Christians do not have to be circumcised ("We should not trouble those Gentiles who are turning to God"; 15:19), *but* that they must observe laws about food purity and sexual relations (15:20). From the point of view of Jewish Christians, this would have been seen a minimal requirement that would have at least permitted table fellowship between Jewish and Gentile Christians.

Acts makes it very clear that the conclusions of the Jerusalem council are communicated with the churches in Antioch and the surrounding area (15:22–35). The Jerusalem church even sends its own representatives along with Paul and Barnabas to deliver this important message (Judas and Silas; 15:22). We are told that the members of the church at Antioch "rejoiced" when they heard the letter from Jerusalem (15:31; cf. 21:25). The Acts description of the Jerusalem meeting and its aftermath portrays a young church dealing with conflict well. Writing some twenty-five or thirty years after the event, the author of Acts depicts Paul as a delegate at a council in which the larger church, represented especially by the churches in Antioch and Jerusalem, is able to work together to resolve a problem that might have split it.

The Council according to Galatians

"In Response to a Revelation"

In comparison to the above, Paul's account of the Jerusalem council in Galatians 2 (written later, during his third missionary journey; see chapter 8) is a kind of reality check about how the early church operated. His account is different in several important ways. Although he is accompanied by Barnabas (and Titus), Paul does not mention that he is a representative of the church at Antioch (2:1). Instead, Paul says that he went up "in response to a revelation" as a way of testing the legitimacy of his ministry (2:2). The same revelation of God that he encountered in Jesus Christ (1:12, 15) is now calling him to confirm and define his mission in relationship to the leaders of the Jerusalem church.

As we might anticipate, Paul himself is the focus of the story. Unlike the open meeting described in Acts, Paul speaks only about a "private meeting" between himself and the "acknowledged leaders" in the church, a way of addressing Peter, James, and John that foreshadows even more negative language later in the passage (Gal. 2:2; see esp. v. 6). Paul does refer to what was probably an earlier encounter between himself and the Judaizers in Antioch, but his words are much sharper than what we hear in Acts (15:2). He did not allow Titus, a Greek, to be circumcised, even in the face of opposition from "false brothers" who were "secretly brought in" in order "to spy on the freedom" of Gentile Christians (Gal. 2:4–5). The intensity of the situation is not left to our imaginations! According to Paul, the very "truth of the gospel" is at stake (2:5).

The result of Paul's private meeting with the "pillars" of Jerusalem (2:9) is, as Paul phrases it, that they "put no obligations on me" (my translation, Gal. 2:6. NRSV: "contributed nothing to me"). This is Paul's way of saying that Peter, James, and John affirmed the message of freedom he had been proclaiming to Gentiles. Circumcision is not required. Nor is there any mention of the legal requirements for Gentiles that figure so prominently in the Jerusalem council as recorded in Acts (i.e., food purity, sexual purity, Acts 15:20). Here again, Paul's Letters and Acts appear to be irreconcilable; it is hard to imagine that the same Paul who affirms that "nothing is unclean in itself" (Rom. 14:14; cf. 1 Cor. 8:1–13) could have accepted James's decree about foods (Acts 15:20). According to Paul, the acknowledged leaders recognize his unrestricted call to the Gentiles and affirm their own ministries to Jews (Gal. 2:8–9). They give Paul the "right hand of fellowship" and ask only that he and his churches remember the poor in Jerusalem (which Paul did; see 1 Cor. 16:1–4; Rom. 15:25–33).

Peter's Hypocrisy in Antioch

Paul does not say anything about an emissary being sent from Jerusalem to Antioch after the conference, but his story too includes an "afterword" in Antioch, although for quite different purposes. Paul apparently returns to Antioch soon after the meeting in Jerusalem, and Peter pays the church a visit as well. What happens there infuriates Paul. When Peter first arrives at the church, he regularly eats with Gentile Christians in a way that is consistent with the conclusions of the Jerusalem council (Gal. 2:12). No food regulations keep Jewish and Gentile Christians from dining with one another. But when "people . . . from James" arrive, Peter withdraws and refuses further table fellowship with Gentiles because he is afraid of this "circumcision faction" (2:12). Other Jewish Christians at Antioch, including

Barnabas, join Peter in this "hypocrisy" (2:13). The effect, of course, is that the church at Antioch is split in two. Jewish Christians, following Peter's example, refuse to be made "unclean" by associating and eating with Gentile Christians. Gentile Christians probably feel either alienated from their Jewish sisters and brothers or compelled (see Paul's use of this word in v. 14) to submit to the law.

Paul says that he opposed Peter to his face and before the entire church (2:11, 14). Once again, as in 2:5, Paul claims that the "truth of the gospel" is at stake (2:14). Paul's rebuke of Peter begins in 2:14 and probably continues in the following verses, although it is difficult to know where his words to Peter end and his instructions to the church at Galatia begin. What Paul says, in essence, is that Jesus Christ, and not the law, is the path to justification with God (2:16). Why would Jewish Christians demand that Gentiles follow torah (2:14) when they themselves know (or should know) that "no one will be justified by the works of the law" (2:16)? The "truth of the gospel" that Paul must defend against Peter's hypocrisy is that the only indispensible thing in God's plan for salvation is faith in Jesus Christ (2:16). Paul knows that God's law has great value, and he continues to wrestle with its place in the Christian life throughout his career (see Gal. 3:19–26; Rom. 7). But this early incident with Peter at Antioch convinces him that Gentiles cannot be compelled to keep the law as if it were the center of the story of salvation. As Paul says with such clarity in Galatians 2:21, "If justification comes through the law, then Christ died for nothing."

This incident with Peter at Antioch has a significant impact upon Paul's missionary career. It probably marks the beginning of less cordial relations with both the church in Antioch and the church in Jerusalem. Apart from Galatians, the church at Antioch is not mentioned in the undisputed letters of Paul.[1] The sarcasm with which he refers to the leaders of the Jerusalem church in Galatians 2:1–10 is a good indication of how he feels about them when he writes this letter (i.e., 55 CE). And Paul mentions Barnabas only once in passing in all of his letters (1 Cor. 9:6). Interestingly, Acts confirms the split between Paul and Barnabas, although it gives quite different reasons for it. According to Acts 15:36–40, the two have a "sharp" disagreement over the participation of John Mark, who had left them during their first journey (13:13). On the positive side, Paul's participation in the Jerusalem council and his spat with Peter in Antioch affect his ministry powerfully, both in terms of how he thinks about the church and how he thinks about salvation in Christ. In the account of the Jerusalem council in Galatians 2, we see Paul's essential theology being born, one that he continues to define the rest of his career. If God's first great revelation to Paul occurs on the road to Damascus, then the second happens here in the midst of church conflict. As Jewish and Gentile Christians vie to establish rules of conduct for the church, Paul is allowed to see two foundational truths: (1) Justification with God comes not through the law but through faith in Christ. (2) Because Christ, and not the law, lies at the center of the faith, the church is one; in him, human ways of dividing between individuals and groups no longer exist (Gal. 3:28).

Paul for Today

A United Church

The Acts account of the Jerusalem council is a portrait of Paul working within an orderly and unified church. It might surprise you to hear me say that Paul's account of the events in Galatians also affirms a high view of the church for the apostle. Yes, there are tensions between Paul and the church at Antioch and the church at Jerusalem. It is likely that Paul was no longer officially "sponsored" by Antioch after their falling out. And the sarcasm we hear when Paul speaks of the leaders in Jerusalem is unmistakable. But Paul's Letters clearly indicate that he remains a member in good standing with the larger church. He continues with a collection for the poor in the Jerusalem church (Rom. 15:25–28). He visits the church there, even though he knows it may be dangerous (Rom. 15:30–33). And Paul elsewhere refers to Peter in ways that indicate a high regard for his leadership in the larger church (see 1 Cor. 1:12; 3:22; 15:5).

But the key indicator of Paul's love for the church in Galatians 2 is the way he boldly fights for inclusion of Gentiles with no strings attached. Life in Jesus Christ is one of freedom, not slavery to a system of laws (2:4; 5:1–12). Gentiles cannot be compelled to submit to law as if it were the ultimate litmus test for Christianity. Paul knows that demanding circumcision and food laws will endanger the unity of the church. Peter's retreat from Gentile believers divides the church in two, one observant and one "unclean." Paul's reaction to Peter's inconsistency might seem shrill until we realize what is at stake. The church is "one" in Jesus Christ (Eph. 4:4, 15); we must "speak the truth in love" (4:15) to ensure this essential unity.

For me, Paul's high regard for the unity of the church in Jesus Christ is one of the most important messages that we in the contemporary church can hear. As stated in the first chapter: *Our transformation through Christ shapes us into people who are capable of love and who seek Christian community.* In later chapters we will discuss the ways he affirms fellowship and community in local congregations, another way of thinking about church unity. But Paul's actions in Jerusalem and Antioch show that the unity of the greater church is also a prime concern. Think of the ways Christians throughout the world divide themselves from one another! One of the greatest shames in Christendom is the way we gather into exclusive groups and denominations, convinced that our theology and Christian practice are superior. There are churches that are exclusive based on race, ancestry, gender, sexuality, income, education, church music, the sacraments, leadership and personalities, political issues, church polity, attitudes toward the Bible, theology, methods of prayer and worship, and so on. Almost every conceivable distinction between Christians becomes a pretext for division. This is hardly the "unity of the Spirit in the bond of peace" that Ephesians speaks about so eloquently (4:3).

It's not that the issues dividing us are unimportant. Many of them are central to how we worship, how we relate to one another in the church, and how we relate to the world. We need to honestly and openly discuss them. But we must not break communion with other congregations or denominations or groups as if we were superior to them or did not need them. Paul's words about "discerning the body" (1 Cor. 11:29) were written about tensions within a specific congregation, but surely they apply to the world church as well. We must discern the body in the sense that we need to recognize Christ's body and blood shed for us, the essential act of redemption that links all believers together. But we must also discern the body in that we affirm the *church* as "the body of Christ" (1 Cor. 12:27). Christ must not be divided! And we need the gifts that our fellow Christians have; the church is like a body in that none of its parts is indispensible (12:12–26). We so often act like eyes that have no need of hands, or heads that have no need of feet!

I know well how cozy our local Christian communities can be, places where most everyone thinks like us and lives like us. And this isolation fits seamlessly with our postmodern world. But I also know the joy I have felt when I encounter Christians from supposedly alien denominations or groups and suddenly realize that they too know Christ! It's like finding a long-lost brother or sister! The family is much bigger than we thought possible! Paul's struggle to have a unified Jewish and Gentile church is one of the best examples in the New Testament of the danger of making our pet issue the definitive one, to the exclusion of all other Christians who disagree with us.

Forgiveness or Justification?

For Jews and Jewish Christians of Paul's day, the theological term "justification" often took on the meaning of "acquittal" in a legal sense.[2] Picture a courtroom: a defendant could be declared either "guilty" or "just" (not liable for punishment) by a judge. In the Jewish religious context, and especially one in which law is central, justification often became a synonym for "forgiveness." Humans fail to do what God requires in the law, but God graciously justifies them or forgives them of their sins. Jewish Christians, of course, see the death and resurrection of Jesus Christ as the sacrifice or the atoning action of God that makes this forgiveness possible.

The remarkable thing about Paul's language of salvation is how little he talks about forgiveness of sins. When he speaks about justification through Christ, his concern is usually something even more radical and transformative. Part of the clue to what Paul means by justification comes in its negative opposite, "not by works of the law" (Gal. 2:16, 21; 3:1–29; 5:3; Rom. 2:20–21, 27–28; 4:1–25; 7:7–25). Paul has learned from his conflicts with Jewish Christians over the years that making the law an entrance requirement for Gentiles challenges the priority of Christ (Gal. 2:21; 3:2–5; 5:4). But this missionary and former Pharisee sees other problems with the law as well.

Mandates about the law often split the church, as we saw above. In Galatians, Paul talks about the curse of the law (3:10, 13), and how the law enslaves us like a prison guard (3:22–24; see section "Ignorant Obedience" in chap. 2). Paul even compares life under the law to the enslavement we experience under the "elemental spirits," the anti-God powers that dwell in the universe (4:3, 9; see chap. 2, "An Evil World"). Paul's statements about the law in Romans are more moderate, but even there he speaks about the law enticing us to Sin (7:7–8).

The one who was a law enforcer among the Pharisees comes to an amazing conclusion: keeping the law cannot save us, nor does breaking the law (accumulating sins) represent the heart of our alienation from God. Salvation is more than simply a matter of forgiveness of sins! Rather, it is God's way of responding to the deep gulf that separates us from him, our hostility toward God, and the control that the cosmic powers of evil exercise over us. Paul replies to the Jewish Christian teachers bothering his Gentile churches by employing their term, "justification," but by using it in quite a different way. He gives the term a meaning more consistent with its Old Testament roots. Justification is God's act of putting humans right with him within the covenant relationship. In both Galatians and Romans, Abraham is Paul's favorite example: "Abraham believed God, and it was reckoned to him as righteousness" (i.e., as one justified;[3] Gal. 3:6; Rom. 4:3; Gen. 15:6). Following Paul's train of thought in Galatians, God's justification through faith is now given to Gentiles through Christ, the one true "offspring" or heir of this promise to Abraham (3:8, 15–16). Because we are in Christ, we Gentiles have become adopted children, heirs of the same justification Abraham received (3:25–4:7). And Paul makes it clear that law plays a secondary role in this drama of salvation. It came 430 years after God's promise to Abraham (Gal. 3:17; cf. Rom. 4:9–12). Its roles as warden and disciplinarian are left behind when Christ appears (Gal. 3:22–24).

We are justified in Jesus Christ! Justification goes far beyond forgiveness of our individual sins. It means that God has reestablished a relationship with us where tremendous barriers to that relationship existed. In Christ, we are changed people. To use Paul's more apocalyptic language, we are "a new creation" (2 Cor. 5:17). We have been empowered to resist the evil powers in the world (Eph. 2:1–10).

We have been simultaneously freed from the burden of the law (Gal. 4:31–5:6), and as new people in Christ, we are freed to serve and love one another (Gal. 5:13).

I think Paul's understanding of salvation in Christ is one of the most important messages that contemporary Christians can hear. When I speak before church groups and hear people discuss the issues in their Christian lives, it is common for them to assess their faith primarily in relationship to the law or some modern equivalent of it. Some people are acutely aware of their sins, the ways they have failed to keep God's law, and are almost obsessed with the constant need to ask God for forgiveness. I sometimes wonder how our weekly confession of sins at worship, wrongly perceived, contributes to the understanding that Christianity is above all an efficient and timely way to be absolved of the punishment for transgressions. We know we'll sin again in the days that follow, but next Sunday will bring yet another opportunity to wipe the slate clean! Others, at the opposite end of the scale, feel some victory in their religious lives, but they measure it primarily on their ability to be "good." They have disciplined themselves to keep the Ten Commandments, to tithe, to pay their taxes, to be good parents and good neighbors, to be loyal Americans, and so on.

Yes, asking God for forgiveness should be a part of every Christian's life. In the New Testament forgiveness is perhaps the most common way of expressing what happens to us in Christ. Seeking forgiveness for our sins demonstrates our humility before God and our need for the ongoing sustenance and empowerment only he can provide. But Paul's revelation must also be heard. We are justified! God has reconciled us to himself, overcoming immense barriers. God loves us as his own children. In Christ we are new people, changed people! Sin and its corollary death, remnants of an age soon to pass, no longer control our destinies (1 Cor. 15:55–56). God has done so much more than just forgive us. In Christ we experience God's love, and God gives us the ability to love others. If we have any ability to do good, it is because God has remade us in the image of Christ (Rom. 6:1–8). Picture the courtroom scene we used earlier in the chapter. God as judge not only acquits us, guilty though we are, but the judge also invites us home to be part of his family: he rehabilitates us! Paul's understanding of justification lies at the heart of what makes Christianity a joyful, liberating experience for me; we can give up on our projects of self-salvation and quit worrying that we have failed to ask forgiveness for some unknown infraction of the law. God loves us as we love our children, and nothing can separate us from this love (Rom. 8:31–39).

Questions for Discussion

1. How is it important to you that you are a member of a larger, worldwide church? What difficult issues challenge the unity of the church catholic (universal) in the present?
2. How do you normally think about the nature of Christ's saving action? Which of the following has been most meaningful for you: forgiveness, justification, redemption, sacrifice, reconciliation, love, and so forth?
3. What is the equivalent to "works of the law" in your life? What are the common markers of a "good" or "successful" life?

7

Paul's Second Missionary Journey

Biblical Texts: Acts 15:40–18:22; 1 Thessalonians

Paul as an Independent Missionary

After his conflict in Antioch (Gal. 2:11–14), it is probably best to see Paul as an independent missionary, one who is not bound to any sponsoring congregation. Nor does he feel comfortable being supported by a congregation while he is ministering there (1 Cor. 9:14–15). What we have come to call Paul's second missionary journey is found in Acts 15:40–18:22. It would be wise to read the account with a map in hand to get a sense of the scope of his travels. Even with Rome's famous roads,[1] travel for a common person was strenuous and dangerous, and you will be amazed at the miles Paul covers. The itinerary for this period (i.e., 50–52 CE) in Paul's life comes almost completely from Acts, although Paul's Letters do confirm many of the places, people, and episodes mentioned in Acts. It is during this second journey that Paul founds the churches to which he would write the letters that are preserved in the New Testament, 1 Thessalonians, Galatians, 1 Corinthians, 2 Corinthians, Philippians, and Philemon. Of these, only 1 Thessalonians, the oldest book in the New Testament, was actually written during the second journey (ca. 51 CE).

Paul in Europe

"Come to Macedonia"

Paul, now with Silas (Acts 15:40) and soon joined by Timothy (16:1), begins by visiting some of the churches founded on his first journey, those in Syria, Cilicia, Derbe, and Lystra (15:41–16:1). Paul's Letters repeatedly mention Timothy as a fellow missionary (Rom. 16:21; 1 Cor. 4:17; 16:10; 2 Cor. 1:1, 19; Phil. 1:1; 2:19; etc.). The account of Paul circumcising Timothy is hard to reconcile with what Paul says elsewhere (Gal. 2:3; 5:6), even though Timothy is a Jew. This act, coupled with the following statement about Paul delivering the results of the Jerusalem council to the churches he visits (Acts 16:4–5), illustrates once again the desire in Acts to present the church as a unified body.

Paul's entrance into Macedonia and his mission at Philippi present two themes that the author of Acts repeats again and again: Paul's guidance and empowerment by the Spirit and how he works within the framework of Roman law. Paul and his group travel through Phrygia and Galatia in central Asia Minor, strengthening the churches in the faith (16:5, 6). Paul may well have founded the churches he addresses in Galatians at this time, although Acts is silent about them. The Holy Spirit forbids them to evangelize in Asia, the Roman province in western Asia Minor (Acts 16:6, 7), but God opens another door. During the night at Troas, Paul has a vision of a man from Macedonia pleading to him, "Come over to Macedonia and help us" (16:8–10). Assuming this vision to be from God, Paul and his party sail from Troas and later arrive at Philippi, the first of several important Macedonian and Greek cities to which they would minister (Thessalonica, Athens, and Corinth). The Spirit's work can also be seen in the earthquake that frees Paul and Silas from prison and leads to the jailer's conversion (16:16–34; cf. 12:6–11). Over and over we see in Acts that God's plan for the proclamation of the gospel is irrepressible.

We also see in Philippi the first of several times when Paul appeals to his status as a Roman citizen (16:35–39). Here, magistrates are forced to apologize for their outrageous treatment of him. Roman citizenship, a status protected by Roman law, gives Paul a tremendous

advantage in his missionary work (see 22:25–29). After his imprisonment in Jerusalem, Paul the Roman citizen is given the opportunity to
defend the gospel before the Judean rulers Felix, Festus, and Agrippa
(23:26–26:32). Roman law honors Paul's appeal to the emperor
(25:11–12), and so Paul's desire to preach in Rome is fulfilled (Rom.
15:22–29), although in quite a different way than he might have
expected! God uses even the Roman Empire to his advantage. One
message for the Gentiles addressed in Luke-Acts is that Christians do
not have to assume that their faith will be in conflict with Roman rule.

Paul's Letter to the Philippians, probably written much later, during
his imprisonment in Rome (60–63 CE), shows that this congregation
is perhaps the least troubled and the most loving of all the churches
Paul founds (Phil. 4:15–20; see discussion in chap. 10). It has been
suggested that the church's stability results from a long-term ministry
by one of Paul's fellow missionaries, the "loyal companion" referred
to in Philippians 4:3.[2] Is this the person who writes the famous "we
passages," the first-person plural narrative beginning in Acts 16:10 and
again in 20:5? The long gap between their initial activities together
in Philippi (16:10–16) and the continuation of the first-person report
when Paul arrives again in Philippi some seven years later (20:5) may
indicate that this fellow missionary stayed in Philippi that whole time.
If this eyewitness is also the author of Luke and Acts, as many scholars
claim, then his long ministry away from Paul might be a way to explain
some of the discrepancies between Acts and Paul's Letters. Perhaps he
wasn't around Paul during the major part of his missionary career and
during the time he wrote most of his letters.

Thessalonica and Beroea

After leaving Philippi, Paul and his group travel east to Thessalonica.
Using his typical approach, Paul preaches in the synagogue on three
Sabbaths and has some success among both Jews and Gentiles (Acts
17:1–4). Unfortunately, he also encounters the now typical hostility
from Jews in the area. They stir up a mob and bring Jason, Paul's host,
before the authorities (17:5). Describing the missionaries as "those
people who have been turning the world upside down" (17:6), the
Jews make a charge that would certainly have caught the attention of

government officials: Paul's message is treason against the empire; Jesus, and not the emperor, is king (17:6–7)! We get a clear sense of how dangerous and radical people felt Christianity to be.

Paul and Silas flee to the city Beroea to avoid the mob and their charges, but the scenario repeats itself. They have considerable success among both Jews and Gentiles in that city, but hostile Jews follow him from Thessalonica (some 50 miles away) and again incite the crowds (17:13). Believers once more escort Paul out of town, this time as far as Athens (17:15). Silas and Timothy remain in Macedonia, however, to minister to the young congregations in Philippi, Thessalonica, and Beroea (17:14).

Perhaps only a few months after being forced to leave Thessalonica, Paul writes the church a letter, our 1 Thessalonians. It is the oldest of all the documents in the New Testament (ca. 51 CE?). One of the fascinating things about the letter is that it corroborates much of what Acts says about Paul's trip to Macedonia. Consistent with Acts, Paul speaks of his shameful treatment in Philippi (1 Thess. 2:2). Like Acts, he mentions Athens as the next stop after Thessalonica and Beroea (1 Thess. 3:1). And especially, Paul confirms that Timothy (and Silas) stayed behind in Thessalonica. In 3:2 Paul talks about how he sent[3] Timothy "to strengthen and encourage" the church in the face of persecutions they were facing (3:3, 4, 7; 2:14). After noting some of the historical tensions between Paul's Letters and Acts, it is wonderful to see an instance where the two are in strong agreement. Paul writes 1 Thessalonians after Timothy has rejoined him, probably in Corinth (Paul's next stop; see Acts 18:5), and a very important part of the letter is simply communicating the joy he (Paul) feels in knowing that they have remained firm in the faith (1 Thess. 3:6–10). The other central concern of the letter, what happens to Christians when they die, will be dealt with below in the "Paul for Today" section.

Athens and Corinth

In Athens Paul preaches in both the synagogue and the marketplace (Acts 17:17), but it is clear that the Gentile audience is of prime importance. Here we see another example of Paul's contextual preaching, this time to non-Jews who nevertheless are "extremely religious" and curious intellectually (17:21–22). Paul begins with what his hearers know. He explains their inscription "to an unknown god" (17:23) by talking about the God of Israel, the creator God, who cannot be contained or controlled by humans (17:24–26). Paul even uses quotations from the philosophers rather than Scripture to support his argument (17:28). And the apostle apparently "has" his audience until he speaks about a man sent by God to judge the world, a man whom God confirms "by raising him from the dead" (17:31). Here Paul's sermon becomes too strange for these sophisticated Gentiles! In a culture where existence after life was usually defined in terms of the soul fleeing the body, imagine how outrageous it would have been to hear someone preach about dead bodies coming to life. The Athenians' reaction to the concept of resurrection in Acts is entirely consistent with issues found in 1 Thessalonians and 1 Corinthians. In both, Paul spends a good deal of time trying to explain what resurrection is, when it happens to Christians, and above all, why it is a good thing (1 Thess. 4:13–5:11; 1 Cor. 15).

According to Acts, Corinth is Paul's last major stop on his second missionary journey (18:1–17). The assertion in Acts that Paul stays there a year and a half (18:11; second in length only to his three-year stay in Ephesus; 20:31) fits well with the complex relationship between Paul and the Corinthians expressed in his letters 1 Corinthians and 2 Corinthians. Paul knows these people and their problems well. Acts tells us that it is at Corinth that Paul meets Aquila and Priscilla,[4] a Jewish Christian couple who have recently been forced out of Rome by the emperor Claudius.[5] They become some of Paul's closest friends and fellow missionaries: in 1 Corinthians 16:19 Paul sends greetings to the Corinthian church from the couple who are with him in Ephesus (1 Cor. 16:8). Later, in his Letter to the Romans, Paul's greeting to the two indicates that they have returned to Rome and have become leaders in the church there (16:3). Other Corinthian Christians found in Acts are also named in Paul's Letters to Corinth; Crispus, who is baptized by Paul (Acts 18:8; 1 Cor. 1:14), and Sosthenes, who apparently becomes part of Paul's missionary group (Acts 18:17; 1 Cor. 1:1). Certainly the most important historical reference in the Acts description of Paul's visit to Corinth is found in Acts 18:12–17. There we are told that a Jewish mob brings Paul before the current proconsul of Achaia, a man named Gallio. Gallio held the office of proconsul for two years, 51–52 CE, so Paul must have been in Corinth at that time. In spite of the many historical tensions between Acts and Paul's Letters, most scholars think that this reference to Gallio is the place to start when dating Paul's career.

The Acts account of Paul visiting Philippi and Thessalonica and Corinth gives almost no information about the congregations established in those places; for that we need to turn to the letters the apostle wrote to these churches. This is especially so concerning the Corinthian correspondence. Paul writes a series of letters to the church there, the content of which has been collected into our two canonical letters, 1 Corinthians and 2 Corinthians.[6] These were written some two to five years after Paul's first visit (Acts 18) during his so-called third missionary journey (54–57 CE).

Paul's second journey is completed by visits to Ephesus, Caesarea, Jerusalem, and then back to Antioch (Acts 18:18–22). Note that Priscilla and Aquila become part of his missionary entourage (18:18).

Paul for Today

Paul the Pastor

What characteristics make Paul a good pastor? Of course, he is first and foremost a missionary, and that is the focus of the narrative in Acts. But Paul's Letters open up a whole other world, one in which Paul not only establishes churches but also cares for them and gets deeply involved in their spiritual and social issues. The following are some of Paul's most important traits as a pastor, and I think we would do well to look at them as we try to understand the task of ministry in the contemporary world.

As we have seen in Galatians, Paul is, above all, a man who is called by God to his ministry (Gal. 1:15–16). He is secure in the knowledge that his proclamation is God's truth (Gal. 1:6–9). He does not waver when he confronts opponents or problems in the church (2 Cor. 11:12–15). He is willing to suffer for the gospel (2 Cor. 4:7–12; 11:22–29) and gives of himself freely to his churches (1 Cor. 9:15–18). The authorization that comes from being transformed and led by the risen Christ is foundational for all those who would enter pastoral ministry.

The second thing to note about Paul the pastor is that he realizes he is a servant, a servant of God and of the people in his congregations (1 Cor. 3:1–9). The tensions in the church at Corinth caused by the people's desire to make their preachers into prima donnas (1:17–2:5) help Paul to understand that neither he nor any other pastor can be the focus of the message. Boasting about human leaders (3:21) and their wisdom and power distorts the message of the cross (1:18). In the case of the Corinthians, it is the congregation, not the preachers themselves, that seeks to make its leaders into superstars. But either way, whether because a church longs for star power or because a pastor is filled with pride, the congregation is transformed into a personality cult. The contemporary church desperately needs pastors who understand their role in the order of things; they are called to humbly serve, to plant, and to water, but only God gives the growth (3:7).

The third notable characteristic of Paul's pastoral ministry is his deep love for the churches he serves. He is not content simply to establish churches, but he seeks an ongoing relationship with them. Perhaps the best proof of this is the large portion of the New Testament attributed to him: Paul writes letters. In Paul's day, letters were an expensive form of communication, and they show just how serious Paul is about nurturing these young congregations.[7] I've always felt that the First Letter to the Thessalonians is an especially moving example of Paul's pastoral love. Look at the letter's thanksgiving (1:2–10). Although thanksgivings were a typical part of a first-century letter, I get no sense that this is just polite language. Paul is filled with the joy that is born of Christian fellowship! Love for these young Christians makes his life a constant prayer for their welfare! The same is true about Paul's words after Timothy's return from Thessalonica (3:6–10). "How can we thank God enough," Paul asks, "for all the joy that we feel before our God because of you?" (3:9). The apostle shows us that pastoral ministry is more than simply obeying a call to serve. It is about pastors genuinely loving their congregations as God has loved them.

The fourth important trait of a pastor modeled by Paul is a willingness to discipline individuals and congregations. Paul writes the

Corinthians as a father admonishing his children (1 Cor. 4:14). In part, admonishment refers to encouragement. Paul reminds the Corinthians who they are in Christ and invites them to imitate him (4:16–17). But admonishment, as Paul uses the term, also refers to a parent's willingness to show a child where she or he is wrong, with punishments in place if necessary. He asks the arrogant at Corinth whether they want him to visit as a father carrying a stick for punishment (4:21)! In the very next section, Paul expands his authority as a disciplining parent by condemning both an incestuous relationship and a church that fails to show its members what it means to live the Christian life (5:1–8). As is the case in families, church discipline is such a costly, messy thing that it only occurs when people are deeply committed to one another. What does it say about our love for one another when no one, not even our pastoral leader, disciplines us when we go astray?

Finally, I think Paul models so well what it means to be a pastoral theologian. Much of what Paul says in his letters is a theological response to congregational issues. First Thessalonians is a case in point. Apart from a chance to express his love for them, Paul writes this letter to answer what was a disturbing question for these Gentiles: what happens to Christians who die before Christ returns (4:13–5:11)? Paul uses the issue to teach and to comfort. When Christ returns, Paul says, "the dead in Christ will rise first" (4:16), and they, along with those who are still alive, "will be with the Lord forever" (4:17). Paul is able to respond with a theological answer that would have been tremendously comforting to those who did not understand resurrection. Christ is stronger than death! Christians do not "grieve as others do who have no hope" (4:13). And Paul the pastoral theologian proceeds to speak about Christ's return as it impacts the present (5:1–10). The "when" of Christ's return, the coming of the proverbial "thief in the night" (5:2, 4), is not as important as living in the light (5:4–8). Paul is astute enough not only to answer the Thessalonians' questions simply and directly, but also to shift the focus to what is central, the comfort of our salvation in Christ and how we live in that salvation (5:8–11). This ability to think theologically about issues in the church and the Christian life is perhaps Paul's greatest gift. He is certainly the father of all those in ministry who pursue the theological life of the mind.

The Pastoral Thinker Today

This is by no means an exhaustive list, but it is an important one. Paul, called and transformed by God, ministers by serving, loving, disciplining, and speaking theologically, applying the teachings of Scripture and tradition to the concrete issues in the church. Although all of these pastoral characteristics are vital, is there one that is especially important in the contemporary church, perhaps one that we more often than not see missing in our pastoral leadership? I could answer that question in several ways. In my experience, many pastors have a difficult time truly loving their congregations, and congregational discipline is certainly not a common thing in mainstream denominations. But perhaps the trait most absent and most needed in the contemporary church is that of *pastoral thinker,* or *theologian.* As individuals, congregations, and denominations, we are bombarded with issues that demand clear thinking and a solid grasp of Bible/theology. You know the list. As denominations we face issues of finance, polity, leadership, sexuality, eroding membership, and so on. As congregations and individuals, we are confronted by these as well as by more personal issues, the loss of loved ones, unemployment, crises of faith, conflicts between members of a church, and so forth. Churches need leaders who are both pastorally sensitive and theologically sophisticated.

There are many reasons for the absence of pastor as theologian in the contemporary church, several of which grow out of current definitions of ministry. If the pastor is primarily a manager, leading and administering and promoting growth much the same way a CEO would in a corporation, then there won't be much time for theological reflection. But what we really need, as Paul shows us, is a definition of ministry that is much more nuanced. Yes, pastors are managers. But far more important, they are those who bring God's message of salvation to the pain and brokenness in the church. Pastoral theologians teach and preach the Bible. They know and apply their theological tradition. Their insights grow out of their own spiritual struggles. Just as important, they know the world well enough to understand both the good and evil it can bring to our lives. Above all, pastoral theologians help their parishioners understand how the good news in Jesus Christ addresses their experience of life. Christianity is a word of truth, and pastors need the God-given wisdom to make that truth real in the everyday lives of church members.

The Pastorals (1 and 2 Timothy, Titus) were most probably written after Paul, but they very much reflect his theology, especially in terms of the essentials in ministry. Over and over, these letters remind the young pastor that ministry demands theological content and application. One of my favorite passages is 2 Timothy 3:14–4:5. The author tells Timothy to "continue in what you have learned and firmly believed," including the teachings of the inspired Word, so that this young pastor might be "proficient, equipped for every good work" (3:14–17). He then goes on to list several tasks that assume a *thinking* pastor:

> In the presence of God and of Christ Jesus, who is to judge the living and the dead, and in view of his appearing and his kingdom, I solemnly urge you: proclaim the message; be persistent whether the time is favorable or unfavorable; convince, rebuke, and encourage, with the utmost patience in teaching. For the time is coming when people will not put up with sound doctrine, but having itching ears, they will accumulate for themselves teachers to suit their own desires, and will turn away from listening to the truth and wander away to myths. (4:1–4)

Questions for Discussion

1. If Paul were your pastor, how would you react to him? Of the pastoral characteristics mentioned above, which do you most look for in a pastor?
2. What do you think of my suggestion that what the contemporary church especially needs is pastoral theologians? What are the potential dangers of such a definition of ministry?
3. Why do you think there so often are tensions between pastor and congregation in the contemporary church?

8

Paul's Third Missionary Journey

Biblical Texts: Acts 18:23–21:14; 1 Corinthians; Galatians 3–6; Romans 15:22–33

Ministries New and Old

Paul's so-called third missionary journey is based upon Acts 18:23–21:14. The focus of this period in Paul's career (54–58 CE) is clearly his ministry in Ephesus (19:1–41). Acts tells us that Paul spends three years there (20:31), and it also devotes considerable space to Paul's farewell to the Ephesian elders (20:17–38). Paul also visits churches founded earlier, those in Galatia and Phrygia (Asia Minor; 18:23) and those in Macedonia and Greece (presumably the congregations in Thessalonica, Philippi, and Corinth; 20:1–12). After leaving Macedonia, Paul travels southward along the coast of Asia Minor (Assos, Miletus, Cos, Rhodes, and Patara; 20:13–15; 21:1) en route to Tyre (Syria; 21:2–7), Caesarea (21:7–14), and ultimately Jerusalem (21:15–17). Already in 19:21 Acts makes it clear that Paul desires to go to Jerusalem and ultimately Rome, and the tension around those anticipated visits is an important theme is this section.

Once again, Acts and Paul's Letters fulfill quite different roles concerning this period in Paul's life as a missionary. Acts gives parts of the story and the travel route of this period, while the letters Paul writes during these years give details about his relationship with various congregations. During the third missionary journey, Paul reaches the height of his letter-writing activity: he writes Galatians, at least four letters to the church at

Corinth, and his letter to the church at Rome, written to a church he had not founded. Many details in Paul's Letters confirm the itinerary Acts gives us, as we shall see. What I have always found interesting, perhaps even amazing, about the story of this period in the church in Acts is that it gives us no clue about explosive congregational problems in two of the areas Paul revisits, Galatia and Corinth.

The so-called third journey is a good example of why dividing Paul's work into three segments is somewhat artificial. Notice that Acts makes very little distinction between Paul's travel to Antioch, what we usually say is the end of his second journey (18:22), and his return to Asia Minor (18:23). Paul's long stay in Ephesus (19:1–41) could easily mark that church as his home base after his second journey. And I have often thought that Acts 19:21 is an important signpost for how we might organize the Acts story of Paul. From here on, Paul's face is set toward Jerusalem, and Acts 21:15 moves the reader seamlessly into that city and its impact upon Paul.

Notice also that the first-person plural narrative, the "we passages," begins again in 20:5 and continues on and off throughout the rest of Acts. As we noted in the previous chapter, because the first-person plural stops in Philippi (16:16) and now resumes with Paul's return to Philippi (20:5), it is plausible that the "we passages" were written by someone who stayed to minister in Philippi but now rejoins Paul's traveling group.

Paul in Ephesus

"Strengthening All the Disciples"

Acts mentions Paul's trip through central Asia Minor on his way to Ephesus only very briefly; he goes "through the region of Galatia and Phrygia, strengthening all the disciples" (18:23). The full story comes to us in Paul's letter to the churches in the northern part of the region of Galatia. It is probably during this visit, some four or five years after he founded these churches, that he first realizes the extent of the problem there: Jewish Christians with links to Jerusalem have been telling these Gentile Christians that they must be circumcised and obey the torah. They are teaching the Galatians, in effect, that they must first become Jews before they can become Christians. Paul probably writes his Letter to the Galatians sometime during his three-year stay in Ephesus. It is one of his most passionate letters.

As we saw in chapter 6, Paul uses his call, the affirmation of his gospel at the Jerusalem council, and his dispute with Peter to set the context for his most basic theological affirmation, that humans are "justified not by the works of the law but through faith in Jesus Christ" (Gal. 2:16). He goes on in the rest of the letter to firmly remind these Gentiles that they have already been freed from the law (3:22–25) and are now God's heirs, God's children (3:29–4:7). Becoming enslaved to religious law (3:8–11) and thus making something other than Christ the center of salvation is to be "accursed" (1:8–9). It is to deny the Holy Spirit working within them (3:1–5). No other letter illustrates so clearly the experiences and interpretations that lie at the center of Paul's theology. Acts give no hint about this trouble brewing in Galatia. Did the author of Acts know about these problems? If he did, did he avoid them in order to create a less-conflicted story of the early church? Or, writing some twenty years later, did he assume that the problems in Galatia, tensions between Jewish and Gentile Christians, were no longer a pressing issue in the church?

Links to the Corinthian Correspondence

Before describing Paul's ministry at Ephesus in earnest (19:8–41), Acts relates two incidents where people have only the baptism of John (18:25; 19:3). In the first, a man named Apollos receives more complete instruction about Jesus from Priscilla and Aquila, and he is able to become a powerful preacher in Corinth (18:24–28). In the second, a group of disciples in Ephesus is baptized in Jesus' name and receive the Holy Spirit (19:1–7). The accounts certainly illustrate again the absolute centrality of Jesus Christ. But the first incident also supports several details about Paul's ministry in Corinth. Apollos's teachers, Priscilla and Aquila, are a couple whom Paul met in Corinth (18:2) and who have been traveling with the apostle (18:18). They all continue on to Ephesus in the Acts narrative. In 1 Corinthians, Paul sends greetings to the Corinthian church from Priscilla and Aquila, writing from Ephesus (16:8, 19). Thus both Acts and 1 Corinthians appear to confirm that this letter was written during this stay at Ephesus. And the Acts description of Apollos as an "eloquent man" who goes to Corinth to preach the gospel (18:24, 28; 19:1) also finds support in 1 Corinthians. There Paul addresses divisions in the church, one of which is based on the people's attraction to preachers who speak with "eloquent wisdom" (1:17). Apollos is one of these preachers (1:12), although Paul gives no indication that Apollos himself cultivated this following (3:5–9, 22).

In his letters, Paul's only references to the time he spends in Ephesus focus on the difficulty of the experience. In 1 Corinthians 16:9 Paul states that he has "many adversaries" in Ephesus. In describing the danger he has endured in his ministry in 15:32, Paul tells how he "fought with wild animals at Ephesus."[1] His three-year stay in Ephesus is a time of high stress. Paul realizes that the churches in Galatia are being tempted to give up the centrality of Christ (see above). Just as troubling, he receives word (1 Cor. 1:11; 5:1) that the church at Corinth is falling apart. They are splitting into factions for various reasons, and the unity of the body of Christ is being compromised (see "Paul for Today," below). Paul writes a series of letters to address the community problems at Corinth. The first letter in the series has been lost (see 1 Cor. 5:9). The second letter he writes is our 1 Corinthians, and it is penned toward the end of his time in Ephesus (1 Cor. 16:8). At some point after writing our 1 Corinthians, Paul makes a "painful visit" to Corinth (2 Cor. 2:1), only to discover that things have deteriorated (Acts does not refer to this visit). Other Christian missionaries who deny Paul's authority and teaching have begun to minister to the church at Corinth (Paul calls them "super-apostles"; 2 Cor. 11:5; 12:11). In response to the turn of events, Paul writes his "tearful letter" (2 Cor. 2:4; a letter either lost or perhaps contained in 2 Cor. 10–13), a confrontational letter he knows was painful for the Corinthians to receive.

All of this shows just how difficult Paul's ministry was at times. For many of us, the theological and communal issues at Galatia and Corinth, not to mention the personal attacks, would be a pastor's worst nightmare. I am always amazed at the serenity Paul displays in the midst of the kind of physical and mental anguish that would tear other people apart. He actually comes to realize that his weakness is an opportunity to rely upon the power and grace of Christ. As he says in 2 Corinthians 12:10: "Therefore I am content with weaknesses, insults, hardships, persecutions, and calamities for the sake of Christ; for whenever I am weak, then I am strong."

An Evil Spirit and Roman Law

According to Acts, Paul's ministry in Ephesus follows the now typical approach: he starts by preaching in the synagogue, and after some hostility and rejection by the Jews, puts most of his energy into the Gentile mission (19:8–10). Two stories are the focus of Paul's Ephesus ministry in Acts. Both show alien forces challenging Paul's empowerment, although resolution is attained in quite different ways. In 19:11–12 we are told that Paul continues to do miracles and exorcisms. Jewish exorcists, the seven sons of the priest Sceva, desire this same power and try to do an exorcism in Jesus' name (19:11–14; cf. Simon and 8:18–24). But the evil spirit refuses to budge: it recognizes the power of Jesus and Paul, but not the exorcists' efforts (19:15). The spirit leaps upon them, roughs them up, and drives them from the house "naked and wounded" (19:16). The result is that many, both Jews and Greeks, believe in Jesus and give up their practices of magic (19:17–20). Even an evil spirit can serve the purposes of God!

The other challenge to Paul's power comes from a certain Demetrius and other silversmiths who worry that Paul's ministry will endanger their trade of making idols of the goddess Artemis (19:23–27).[2] An enraged mob comes together to protest Paul's attack on their goddess. Nothing can quiet them until a coolheaded town clerk reminds the crowd of the due process in Roman law and that this same law could charge them with rioting (19:35–41). At these words the mob is dismissed, and Paul is able to go on his way to Macedonia. If an evil spirit can be used by God to further Paul's ministry (above), certainly Roman law also can!

Revisiting Macedonia and Greece and On to Jerusalem

Reconciliation with Corinth

In Acts, the brief account of Paul's travels after leaving Ephesus tells us that he went through Macedonia (via Troas and visiting the churches at Philippi and Thessalonica) to Greece (Corinth, where he spends three months), then back through Macedonia to Troas (20:1–5). What this short description does not detail is Paul's ongoing relationship with the Corinthians, nor does it tell us that while in Greece (Cenchreae, the seaport of Corinth; Rom. 16:1) Paul writes his magnum opus, his letter to the Romans. After writing his "tearful letter," Paul sends Titus to Corinth to minister to them and try to mend the relationship. According to 2 Corinthians 2:12–13, Paul expects to meet Titus again at Troas immediately after leaving Ephesus, but Titus is not there. Paul does unite with Titus in Macedonia, however, and Titus brings wonderful news about repentance and reconciliation with Paul in the Corinthian church (2 Cor. 7:5–16). Paul then writes a beautiful letter of reconciliation before arriving in Corinth (Acts 20:2, 3); it is found in the first part of what is now our 2 Corinthians (1:1–9:15). For a wonderful glimpse of Paul's expression of pastoral joy and the love and the parental pride he has for the congregations he has founded, no passage is more powerful than 2 Corinthians 7:5–16. Paul's last visit to Corinth must have been a joy-filled time!

To Jerusalem and Rome

Probably near the end of his stay in Corinth (or nearby Cenchreae, to be exact; Rom. 16:1), Paul writes his letter to the Christians in Rome. Paul hopes to visit them on the way to further mission in Spain (Rom. 15:22–29). Because Paul had not founded this church, Romans is written to introduce himself and his thought to the Christians there and perhaps to dispel false information circulating about the apostle. The letter falls into well-defined sections that give an insightful overview of Paul's thought at this mature stage of his life. After the introductory parts of the letter (including the typical statement of sender/recipient, 1:1–7; salutation, v. 7b; thanksgiving, vv. 8–15), Paul gives a thesis statement that telegraphs topics he will discuss (1:16–17). The letter, he says, will be about the salvation that comes by faith (1:16). Very much on his mind is the fact that it comes "to the Jew first and also to the Greek" (v. 16). This salvation is, at its essence, a faith-received "righteousness [or justification] of God" (v. 17).[3] Paul carries through with this statement of theme very well. The first section is about humans' Sin, our alienation from God (1:18–3:20). The next section (3:21–8:39) talks about God's response to this alienation through Jesus Christ, using various word pictures to describe how God reestablishes a relationship with humans: redemption (3:24), sacrifice (3:25), reconciliation (5:10–11), adoption (8:15–16), new life in the Spirit (8:1–17), and above all, justification (3:27; 4:1–15, 25; 8:33; etc.). As in Galatians, Paul is concerned with the relationship between Jewish law and salvation in Christ: "A person is justified by faith apart from works prescribed by the law" (Rom. 3:28; also see 4:9–15; 5:18–21; 7:4–25).

The last major section of Romans, 12:1–15:13, is what we might expect after section 2 (3:21–8:39), the human response to God's salvation in Christ. This would then conclude a logical and succinct story of salvation under the headings "guilt, grace, and gratitude."[4] But Paul's letter does not proceed directly from "grace" to "gratitude"; instead he separates the two with a long section on God's plan of salvation for both Jews and Gentiles (Rom. 9–11). We will discuss issues raised in Romans 9–11 in the "Paul for Today" section of chapter 9, but here it is important to stress how telling this part of Romans is in terms of Paul's own situation. In Romans, Paul says he is worried about how he will be treated by unbelievers in Jerusalem and whether his collection for the Jerusalem church will be well received (15:30–33; for the collection see 2 Cor. 8–9; Gal. 2:10). Acts 19:21–22 tell us that Paul is being led by the Spirit to go to Jerusalem and eventually to Rome after his current journey. Much of the last part of the third journey reported by Acts is focused on his visit to Jerusalem. We are told in Acts 20:16 that Paul wants to avoid visiting Ephesus again because he wants to be in Jerusalem by Pentecost. At Miletus he does visit the Ephesian elders, however (20:17), and his extended farewell speech shows his fear of being imprisoned or killed by the Jews in Jerusalem (20:22–25, 36–38). Even in Caesarea, the last leg of his third journey before Jerusalem, Paul is given a prophecy from one Agabus, who says that he will be bound by Jews and handed over to Gentiles (21:10–11). Paul responds that he is ready to be bound and even to die in Jerusalem for the name of Jesus Christ (21:13). Both Paul's letters and Acts communicate his anxiety over the upcoming trip. As Paul sits in Corinth and writes to the Roman Christians, it is surely his anticipated journey to Jerusalem and the conflict it will generate that forces him to wrestle theologically with "to the Jew first and also to the Greek" (Rom. 1:16).

Paul for Today

Barriers to Christian Community in Corinth

As we noted above, Paul's time in Ephesus must have been extremely difficult. He hears that the Corinthian church is experiencing severe internal problems. Various issues are splitting the church apart.[5] The particular barriers to community at Corinth are stunningly like the ones we experience in the modern church. There are factions based on a wrongheaded adoration of certain preachers: "My group is superior because we have a much better preacher" (cf. 1 Cor. 1:10–4:21). Sound familiar? There is immorality in the church, and no one takes action: "I really don't care what they do" (cf. 5:1–6:20)! The church is experiencing tensions over the roles of men and women in the church (cf. 7:1–40; 11:2–16). Christians abuse their freedom and hurt younger or weaker members of the church: "If we are free in Christ, then why do we have to be so careful about how we act?" (cf. 8:1– 11:1). The rich abuse the poor in the Corinthian church (11:17–34), and certain Christians who appear to be more gifted by the Spirit look down upon those who are not (1 Cor. 12–14). Finally, there is a lack of theological unity in the church. Some do not believe that Christians are raised from the dead: "Is this theological issue really important?" (cf. 1 Cor. 15). Which of these barriers to community are present in your church? There is actually an odd sort of comfort that comes in knowing that the early church, so often held up as exemplary, has many of the same issues we now experience.

"Love Builds Up"

As noted in the introduction, *our transformation through Christ shapes us into people who are capable of love and who seek Christian community.* First Corinthians is a wonderful textbook for Christians in terms of how we can address congregational divisions. The people at Corinth are babes in the faith (3:1–4). They pride themselves on their wisdom and strength (4:8–13), when in reality they have not yet shed many of the thoughts and actions that controlled them before they became Christians. If I were to summarize Paul's response to the Corinthians, his words in 1 Corinthians 8:1 would be a good place to start: "Knowledge puffs up, but love builds up." What the Corinthians do not fully understand is how the love of Christ, made most visible to us in his death on the cross, turns our old standards upside down. We cannot champion the wisdom and power of our preachers when Christ came to us in the foolishness of the cross (1:17–2:5). We cannot seek our own freedom in a way that is oblivious to its impact upon our fellow Christians (8:9–13). Because we are *one* in the love of Christ, the world's ways of dividing between people and rewarding people, the world's issues of gender, class, race, and giftedness—these must no longer control us. As Paul says in Galatians 3:28, there responding to divisions based upon the law: "There is no longer Jew or Greek, there is no longer slave or free, there is no longer male and female; for all of you are one in Christ Jesus." In 1 Corinthians 13, Paul makes his clearest statement about the kind of love that governs the church. He speaks about its importance (13:1–3) and its eternity (13:8–13), and most important for our purposes here, the nature of love that Christians practice because they have been transformed by Christ:

> Love is patient; love is kind; love is not envious or boastful or arrogant or rude. It does not insist on its own way; it is not irritable or resentful; it does not rejoice in wrongdoing, but rejoices in the truth. It bears all things, believes all things, hopes all things, endures all things. (13:4–7)

There is no more pressing issue in the contemporary church than that of the absence of love and fellowship, the lack of Christian community in our congregations. I know of many Christians who search for community and can find none. On the other hand, often Christians do not even know that it is something they should expect! Perhaps the best proof of this community problem is the fact that 80 percent of people in this country who claim to be Christian do not consider participation in a church to be a necessary part of their faith.[6] How can we expect to be supported and fed apart from our brothers and sisters in Christ? For Paul, the love he has experienced in Christ *must* find expression among his fellow Christians: church is not optional! And Paul makes it clear that service to his fellow Christians is the ultimate in liberation. In acts of service, Paul is freed from concerns about his welfare and how he might be perceived by others (see 1 Cor. 9). He is freed to love, to incarnate himself in the church he serves (9:19–23). In a society that so often thinks about self, we have a freedom that comes from being in a community where God, and not one's concern about status and image, is the most important thing!

Questions for Discussion

1. Of the several church-splitting issues dealt with in 1 Corinthians (above), which have you most often seen in the church? How did members of the church deal with the problem?
2. What aspects of our culture make the formation of Christian community more difficult?
3. How does Paul's teaching about the message of the cross make participating in Christian community more possible (1 Cor. 1:18–25)?

9

Arrested in Jerusalem
and Imprisoned in Caesarea

Biblical Texts: Acts 21:15–26:32; Romans 9–11; 1 Corinthians 15; 1 Thessalonians 4:13–5:11

"To the Ends of the Earth"

True to Paul's foreboding and the Spirit's predictions, the apostle is arrested in Jerusalem (Acts 21:15–26:32; 58–60 CE). Before he is sent to Rome, most of this time in prison is spent in Caesarea, the seat of the Roman governor. Acts gives us a clear picture of Jewish hostility toward Paul, but it also relates both the reasonableness and spinelessness of the civic rulers he encounters (Lysias, Felix, Festus, and Agrippa). Because of his arrest, Paul is able to witness to Jews and Gentiles in high places. And Paul will go to Rome ("to the ends of the earth," Acts 1:8) to proclaim the gospel there, although the circumstances of his visit are far different than he could have imagined. The other key theme in this section of Acts, I think, is how important and yet problematic the resurrection of Jesus Christ is in Paul's proclamation of Jesus. Paul emphasizes the resurrection of Christ strongly in all of his many speeches. But the rulers he addresses mock the idea (26:24), and even Jews cannot agree that such a thing as resurrection can happen (23:6–10). Think of how difficult it would have been to proclaim a message of salvation whose central tenet is considered by many to be impossible, let alone desirable!

Once again, almost all of the details about this period in Paul's life, most of it in prison, come from Acts. We do know from

Paul's Letters that he anticipates going to Jerusalem and Rome (Rom. 15:22–29). Paul repeatedly writes that one of his reasons for going to Jerusalem is to bring a collection to the poor there (Rom. 15:25–26; 2 Cor. 8–9). We also know that two of his undisputed letters, Philippians and Philemon, are written while he is in prison. Moreover, there is strong confirmation in Paul's Letters of some of the themes presented in Acts 21:15–26:32. In the section "Paul for Today" we will deal with the two mentioned above, that God has a plan for salvation that includes both Jews and Gentiles (Rom. 9–11), and the importance of believers' resurrection (1 Thess. 4:13–18; 1 Cor. 15).

Arrested in Jerusalem

Seized in the Temple

After Paul and his group arrive in Jerusalem, they visit James and the elders, the leaders of the church (Acts 21:17–20). They welcome Paul cordially (21:17), but the bulk of their words have to do with avoiding the wrath of Jewish Christians. We are told that thousands of Jewish Christians who are zealous for the law have heard that Paul does not defend circumcision and the legal traditions among those he converts (Acts 21:20–21). There is a deep rift in Christianity that endangers Paul. James and the elders encourage Paul to take part in a rite of purification that will prove his loyalty to the law (21:23–26).

Paul does purify himself, but Jews from Asia nevertheless stir up the crowd when they see him in the temple (21:27). Paul is accused both of profaning the Jewish traditions and of bringing a Gentile into the temple (21:28–29). A mob forms; they drag Paul out of the temple and begin to beat him (21:30–31). As we have seen before, it is a Roman official who establishes order (21:31–36). This tribune is impressed with Paul's knowledge of Greek and his origin in Tarsus (21:37–39) and, amazingly, grants Paul's request to address the mob (21:40).

Paul's First Defense Speech

This is the first of several defense speeches Paul delivers in this section of Acts (21:40–22:21). It focuses on his radical transformation in

Jesus Christ in a way that is sensitive to his Jewish audience. Speaking in Hebrew,[1] Paul tells his hearers that he is a good Jew like all of them, educated in the law under Gamaliel, and zealous for God (22:3). Trying to emphasize what they have in common, Paul even discloses how he persecuted the church (22:4–5). Paul carefully crafts a message that lets him share about his conversion/call (22:6–16) in the context of his earlier hatred for Christianity. It is hard to imagine a setting more appropriate for this approach. Even Paul's response to a vision from Jesus after his experience on the road to Damascus (recorded nowhere else), a directive that he leave Jerusalem immediately (22:17–21), is an appeal to his audience. Certainly these pious Jews could relate to a speaker who himself imprisoned Christians and took part in the killing of Stephen (22:19–20). But Paul's sophisticated speech falls on deaf ears. As soon as he mentions his call to Gentiles, the people begin to riot again (22:22–23).

The tribune reacts by taking Paul away from the mob. He is tied up and is about to be examined by flogging (!) when Paul asks the centurion whether it is legal to treat an uncondemned Roman citizen in this way (22:25–29). Paul appears to time his question for maximum impact: the tribune is humbled and the soldiers draw back (22:26–29). Once again, Paul's status as a Roman citizen is used to his and the gospel's advantage. Instead of being beaten, Paul is given a chance to respond to his accusers, the Jewish council, or Sanhedrin (22:30–23:10).

Before the Council and Off to Caesarea

In his defense before the Sanhedrin, we see a bold and articulate Paul (23:1–10). He understands that the heart of his message, the resurrection of a human being, is a point of contention even among the Jews. After noting that the council is composed of both Sadducees and Pharisees, Paul makes a statement he knows will divide his accusers: "I am on trial concerning the hope of the resurrection of the dead" (23:6). Unlike the Sadducees, the Pharisees accept the possibility of resurrection, and they quickly take Paul's side against the more conservative members of the council (23:7–9). A violent argument arises, and the tribune must once again remove Paul (23:10). Paul has fulfilled God's plan that he testify to the gospel in Jerusalem, and Rome awaits; God continues to encourage the apostle that he is doing God's will (23:11).

Certainly no human plot can foil the progress of the good news. When forty zealous Jews hatch a plan to kill Paul if he is examined further by the council, God uses Paul's nephew, a perceptive Roman tribune, and 470 mounted and well-armed soldiers to get Paul out of town (23:12–24). Those conspiring against Paul don't stand a chance! The tribune Lysias's introductory letter to the Judean procurator Felix in Caesarea is one of the clearest statements in Acts that Rome and Christianity need not be in contention (23:26–30). Lysias states that Paul is a citizen of Rome, and as such he has the right to be protected from those who accuse him unjustly (23:27–28). The tribune writes that he rescued Paul and that, in his opinion, nothing in the Jews' accusations of Paul constitutes a serious crime (it is all about matters of "their law"; 23:29). Not only is Paul not doing anything against Roman law, but Roman law can also be used to Paul's advantage.

Held in Caesarea

Testimony before Felix

The Acts story about Paul in Caesarea is about his witness to people in high places. When I read this account, I am always reminded of Jesus' prophecy that his disciples "will stand before governors and kings because of me, as a testimony to them" (Mark 13:9). Paul's first defense is before the procurator Felix in response to accusations leveled by Tertullus, a lawyer for the high priest Ananias (Acts 24:1–21). Once again, Paul defends himself extremely well. He says that the Jews in Jerusalem are falsely accusing him, and that they have no evidence against him (24:10–13). As we might expect, the heart of his defense is what is most powerful about "the Way," its affirmation that God has raised a human being from the dead (24:15, 21). Paul also argues that resurrection, a concept that appears to be so disturbing to his opponents in Jerusalem, is entirely consistent with the promises of the Law and the Prophets (24:14–16). The apostle certainly overstates the consensus about human resurrection among the Jews of his day (24:15, a "hope that they themselves also accept"), as we saw in the dispute between the Sadducees and the Pharisees. But the idea that God's Word points forward to a new age characterized by resurrection is very much a part of Paul's thought in his letters (see 1 Cor. 15:20–28 and "Paul for Today," below).

Defense before Festus and Agrippa

None of the rulers mentioned in this section of Acts comes off well, even though they do protect Paul by following Roman law. Felix is intimidated by Paul's words (24:24–25), and he hopes for a bribe for Paul's release (24:26). Festus tries to please the Jews by having Paul go back to Jerusalem (25:9), but Paul knows his rights. The apostle appeals "to the emperor's tribunal," and the wheels are set in order, irreversibly, it seems, for Paul to go to Rome (25:10–12; 26:32). When Festus introduces King Agrippa and Bernice to the case, he actually admits that he has no idea what to write the emperor about Paul (25:25–27). King Agrippa, the ruler with Jewish links that might have given him some insight into the truth Paul is proclaiming, tries to be above any pedestrian commitment. He is most well known for his condescending response to Paul's message: "Are you so quickly persuading me to become a Christian?" (26:28).

Paul's defense before Governor Festus and King Agrippa[2] and his sister Bernice is what could be called a "show trial" (25:23–26:32). The earthly rulers bring all their pomp and ircumstance (25:23). Paul is at his articulate best. This is the last of the long defense speeches of Paul in Acts; it would surely have been held up as a model for how Christians might defend themselves when standing before earthly rulers. Even though Paul is addressing Festus, Agrippa, Bernice, and all the other dignitaries in the hall (25:23), he directs his words especially toward Agrippa, the one with a Jewish background and knowledge (26:2–3). And so this defense, like that in 22:1–21, takes on a Jewish context.

Much as he does in Acts 22, Paul shows that he was raised as a conservative Jew (26:4–11). He reminds Agrippa that he was a strict Pharisee, one thoroughly trained in the law, in order to establish credibility for a potent argument: the hope he has in Jesus Christ is the fulfillment of the promise made by God to the Jews (26:6–7). Paul states the heart of the matter in question form: "Why is it thought incredible by any of you that God raises the dead?" (26:8). The implied answer, of course, is that any good biblical interpreter would *not* see it as incredible. What has happened in Jesus Christ, his resurrection from the dead, is the sign of the coming of God's kingdom that Jews have so long anticipated. The message Paul proclaims is not some wild deviation from Judaism, but rather a fulfillment of it!

Paul goes on to speak of his persecution of the church (26:9–11), again building on the fact that he is a real Jew who had serious problems with the message of Christ. This report of how he previously hated Christianity makes Paul's report of his conversion/call (26:12–18) seem all the more radical and, I think, believable. What could possibly change a hardened enemy of the church but the voice of the risen Lord himself! This is the third account of Paul's conversion/call in Acts (see 9:1–8; 22:4–16), and the only one that has Jesus say to Paul: "It hurts you to kick against the goads" (26:14). A goad is a stick that is used to prod or direct an animal. The risen Jesus is telling Paul that his hatred of Christianity is a denial of the inevitable; he cannot stand against God's will. And Jesus goes on in this account to detail God's plan for Paul, especially his task among the Gentiles (26:17–18):

> I am sending you to open their eyes so that they may turn from darkness to light and from the power of Satan to God, so that they may receive forgiveness of sins and a place among those who are sanctified by faith in me.

Paul's defense before the dignitaries is that he is simply doing what the Lord told him to do: he is "not disobedient to the heavenly vision" (26:19). His final words emphasize that the revelation he received from Christ is entirely consistent with that found in the Law and the Prophets (26:22–23). Here Paul more fully defines the hope of his ancestors mentioned in 26:6–8. Scripture affirms about the Messiah exactly what Paul himself has been proclaiming, that Christ must suffer, and that, by being the firstfruits of the resurrection, he would become the light of the world, to both Jews and Gentiles (cf. 26:18).

Finally, it's important to note how Paul's defense is both deferential and bold. He pays tribute to Agrippa's knowledge and authority: Paul says he is fortunate to have a judge so familiar with Jewish ways and so secure in his power that he can listen to Paul patiently (26:2–3). But when the opportunity arises, Paul is quick to direct his astounding message even to the rulers. When Festus protests that Paul must be insane, Paul retains his composure, asserting that he is telling the truth (26:25). Even more, he takes the opportunity to drive his prophetic message home to Agrippa, the one ruler there who might understand. "Do you believe the prophets?" he asks King Agrippa. "I know that you believe" (26:27). These dignitaries do not terrify Paul! And after Agrippa's droll response (26:28), Paul has the audacity to claim as his prayer that all those listening might become as he is, "except for these chains" (26:29). Imagine the courage it would take to assert to all the prominent people of the city that he, Paul, a poor itinerant man of faith, might be God's model for remaking them!

Paul's words are favorably received. Agrippa admits that Paul has done nothing wrong (26:31). But the wheels have been set in motion: Paul has appealed to the emperor, and to Rome he must go (26:32). The last two chapters of Acts, with Paul's journey to Rome and his house arrest there, fulfill Jesus' words that his disciples will be his witnesses "to the ends of the earth" (1:8).

Paul for Today

The Resurrection of the Dead

What happens to us as Christians when we die? At most of the funerals I attend, pastors affirm that the departed believer is with Christ. She or he is in heaven. Nothing, not even death, can separate us from God's love. These are wonderfully comforting words, and they find confirmation in Paul's Letters. In Philippians 1:23, Paul talks about his own death and his "desire . . . to depart and be with Christ." In Romans 8, Paul says that God's love for us in Christ is so powerful that not even the worst things we might imagine, including death, can steal it away from us. Still, I often wish that we as pastors would say more about the most basic way that Paul, and indeed most of the New Testament, speaks about life after death: those in Christ will be raised from the dead.

In Acts we have seen how contentious the issue of resurrection is in the ancient world. Gentiles scoff at or are curious about this strange topic (17:17). Not even all Jews accept the possibility that a person could experience a bodily resurrection (23:6–9). Paul brings up the idea of resurrection often because he preaches that Christ has been raised from the dead; unless people accept that resurrection is possible, they certainly won't believe that it has already occurred!

Resurrection is a common topic in Paul's Letters as well, but there the specific issue is *believers'* resurrection. The Gentiles in Paul's churches apparently don't have any trouble accepting that Christ has risen, but trying to fathom their own resurrections is another matter. Paul asserts a necessary link between Christ's resurrection and ours. Jesus Christ is "the first fruits of those who have died," the one whose resurrection is proof that the new age, the time when all believers will be raised, will soon be here (1 Cor. 15:20). In Thessalonica, the problem concerning believers' resurrection appears to be that they have so little information about it (1 Thess. 4:13–18). The Christians there wonder what has happened to their fellow Christians who died before Christ's return. In no uncertain terms, Paul states that because Christ arose, his followers will rise as well (4:14). We do "not grieve as others do who have no hope" (4:13); when Christ returns, "the dead in Christ will rise first" (4:16).

In Corinth, the problem is more serious. There some are denying that people can be raised from the dead (1 Cor. 15:12). Paul makes the link between our resurrection and Christ's absolutely clear. If humans cannot be raised, then Jesus Christ, as a human, could not have been raised, and if Christ has not been raised, then our faith is a sham (15:12–19). Believers' resurrection is not an optional part of Christianity. Paul spends most of his time trying to explain to these Gentile Christians why resurrection of the body is both possible and desirable. The resurrected body will be a "spiritual body" (1 Cor. 15:44). It will be both like and unlike the bodies we now inhabit, just as a seed has both continuity and discontinuity with the plant it produces (15:36–37, 42–43). Our new bodies will be "imperishable," "raised in power," and "bear the image of the man of [from] heaven [Christ]" (15:42–49). But what is raised is still a body. Paul cannot imagine eternal life in bodiless "souls." We will be raised as bodies, as human beings who have identities and who remember our former lives. It will really be you and me! And as new, raised people, people who are given new life in Jesus Christ, we signal the defeat of death and all the other anti-God powers that are still part of this age: "Death has been swallowed up in victory" (15:54–55, 26).

Years ago I taught a class on the Apostles' Creed in a church where I was the visiting pastor. When we came to the clause stating I believe in "the resurrection of the body," none of the longtime church members in that class knew that these words referred to the resurrection of believers; they thought it spoke only of Christ's resurrection! I was amazed. Why is it important that Christians know about resurrection as opposed to simply anticipating "heaven"? For one thing, it defines our hope more clearly. As people raised to new life, we will have both a personal identity and relationships with others. When Paul says in 1 Corinthians 13 that love is the one thing that extends into the future, I believe he is defining the love we will experience both from God and from fellow believers. Christian community will be part of that new bodily existence!

Another reason for emphasizing resurrection is that it points to the importance of the bodies we now have. Thus Paul says to those Corinthians who live in immorality, "Do you not know that your body is a temple of the Holy Spirit within you, which you have from God, and that you are not your own?" (1 Cor. 6:19). Put more broadly, resurrection of the body is a way of saying that God's creation, the world and all that it contains, is a very good thing and worthy of redemption. Obviously the incarnation itself, God's Son assuming human form (Phil. 2:5–11), is the strongest affirmation of God's love for this world. Finally, understanding that resurrection is God's plan for us helps us to realize how seriously God takes death as one of those powers that must be defeated for the new age to dawn. Christ's resurrection is God's promise to us that we will experience a time when "death will be no more" (Rev. 21:4). As both Acts and Paul's Letters affirm, the resurrection of the body is an absolutely essential part of the Christian hope.

God's Plan for Jews and Gentiles

Acts shows Paul's frustration with the Jews' response to the gospel. In fact, the entire book of Acts concludes with Paul's declaring to his Jewish hearers a now-common statement: "Let it be known to you then that this salvation of God has been sent to the Gentiles; they will listen" (28:28). This issue is always close to the surface in Paul's Letters as well. Why, Paul must have wondered, do Jewish Christians and Gentile Christians approach the faith so differently (see Galatians; Phil. 3:2–11)? In terms of coming to Christ, is the Jewish faith an advantage or a liability (Rom. 3:1–20)? What does it mean that salvation in Christ is "to the Jew first and also to the Greek" (Rom. 1:16)? Paul deals with the issue of Jews and Gentiles in God's plan most fully in Romans 9–11.

Paul begins Romans 9–11 by describing the sorrow and anguish he feels because Jews have not widely accepted Jesus Christ (9:2). He would even offer himself to be "cut off from Christ" if somehow that might be a sacrifice that would bring his people to belief (9:3; cf. Exod. 32:32). How can it be that God's chosen people—to whom belong the "adoption, the glory, the covenants, the giving of the law, the worship, and the promises" (9:4)—now appear to be so hardened against the coming of their Messiah?

Paul responds to the dilemma of Jews and Gentiles in God's plan in three ways. His first response is an answer to the implied question that the failure of the Jews to accept Christ raises doubts about God's righteousness (9:6; see 1:17). If Gentiles, rather than Jews, are now recipients of the promises of God made long ago to Jews, what does that say about the trustworthiness of God? Paul's answer is, in effect, that we as humans have no right to question the almighty God (9:20). God chooses and rejects according to his own sovereign will (9:7–15). God is the potter and we are the clay (9:19–21; Jer. 18:6). This argument certainly puts humans in their place! The story of salvation is not ours to critique or even to fully discern. Gods plan "depends not on human will or exertion, but on God who shows mercy" (9:16). This latter clause is very important in Paul's argument here. Even as Paul stresses the sovereignty of God's actions, he also witnesses to a God who seeks to fulfill his promises (9:8–9), especially his desire to show mercy. In 9:22–26 we get a hint of what Paul will say in chapter 11, that God's wrath toward some (9:22) is "to make known the riches of his glory for the objects of mercy" (9:23). What we can know of God's plan for salvation is that now Gentiles, those who formerly were not God's people, are now being called "children of the living God" (9:26; Hos. 2:23).

Paul's second response to the issue deals with God's apparent rejection of his people (Rom. 11:1). Even though it might appear that Jews have rejected Christ, he reminds his readers that he and many other Jews know Christ. These Jews form a "remnant" through which God is working (11:5; cf. 9:27). I have often thought that Paul's reference to Elijah's words are especially for himself. As he anticipates his trip to Jerusalem, he too must have felt like saying: "I alone am left, and they are seeking my life" (Rom. 11:3; 1 Kgs. 19:10, 14). Paul is reminding himself and the Romans that God can work through a chosen few. The promise to the Jews is still alive.

Paul's final response comes in the later half of Romans 11. What he gives us is a "mystery" revealed (11:25), God's plan for Jews and Gentiles sketched in broad strokes. According to Paul, God has hardened Israel "until the full number of the Gentiles has come in" (11:25). Israel is made "jealous" by this inclusion of Gentiles (11:11, 13), and this leads, in turn, to their "full inclusion" (11:12). In the end, "all Israel will be saved" (11:26). The gospel of Jesus Christ comes "to the Jew first," to those who are heirs of the promises, as Paul has affirmed earlier in Romans (1:16). But God's intention is that this message of salvation come to all people, not just Jews. So God allows a hardening of Israel, a temporary rejection of Christ that results in the proclamation of the good news to Gentiles. The Jews' "stumbling means riches for the world" (11:12). But there is one more twist in the plan Paul envisions. After the "full number" of Gentiles has come in (11:25), Israel will come to its senses (according to Paul, out of jealousy; 11:11) and be grafted back into the root (11:23). God will not abandon his chosen people: "The gifts and the calling of God are irrevocable" (11:29).

If you are like me, Paul's vision of God's plan of salvation for Jews and Gentiles raises as many questions as it answers. But I am certain of this: Paul's intention is not to give us details about how and when all this will take place, just as Jesus' words about the return of the Son of Man cannot be used to predict the hour (Mark 13:32). Nor can Paul's words be construed to refer to a reestablishment of the modern State of Israel. The apostle is not speaking about nationhood: he is speaking about how God is working to bring both Jews and Gentiles to the mercy that comes in Jesus Christ.

When God's sovereignty is stressed as strongly as it is in Romans 9–11, we humans quickly reach the limits of our understanding. If God plans and "makes" history, what role do we as humans play? Paul's attempt to explain God's plan for Jews and Gentiles, if even in just its barest form, reminds him just how incomprehensible it all is. God is the potter, we are the clay. I think this is the most essential teaching to emerge from this section of Romans. It's certainly not the case that we can know nothing about God. Paul's words in Romans 9–11 echo what we read everywhere in his letters, that God has a plan for us and that this plan is one of love and mercy. But when it comes to understanding the details of this plan, we stand humbled before God. Paul rightly closes this section of Romans with a salutation expressing God's greatness (11:33):

> O the depth of the riches and wisdom and knowledge of God! How unsearchable are his judgments and how inscrutable his ways!

How does history "move"? Where is it going? Many people, including most Gentile thinkers in Paul's day, assume that history is cyclical. Trends in history come and go, propelled by the ebb and flow of economic and natural events and human leadership. But we as Christians have a quite different view of history. God is leading the universe toward a specific end or goal, one that centers upon his loving relationship with all of creation. Of course, Christianity is not the only religion to have a linear view of history, one with both a beginning and an end, but is there another religion where God has a greater hand in shaping history? God calls Abraham and his chosen people, leads them out of slavery, and sends them the prophets. In the "fullness of time" (Gal. 4) God sends his Son in human form, the ultimate act in history "making." And the Holy Spirit continues to empower and direct God's people, leading them toward eternal life in God's new age. For us, history is the ongoing story of God's involvement in our world for the purpose of salvation.

Paul's discussion of Jews and Gentiles in God's plan points to a significant tension in our Christian lives. He strongly affirms that God is moving history, but he is unable to show how this is so except in the broadest of strokes. Paul cannot tell us how or when the transition from the Jews' exclusion to their inclusion will take place. We too joyfully acclaim God's loving participation in our world, but certainty about the specifics often eludes us. Which events happening around us are of God's doing? Which ones have a more sinister origin? Most of the time, we don't know. As Christians we encounter a tension between our robust proclamation of God's shaping of history, especially in the story of Jesus Christ, and the humbling we experience when we realize how little of God's plan we actually understand. Our "knowing" has significant limitations: we believe, but we cannot "prove." This recognition of what we cannot know about God's plan is surely one of Paul's most important teachings in Romans 9–11 for the contemporary church, in which we are often far too quick to claim that we know how a certain war or natural disaster is being used by God. Humility goes hand in hand with a confident faith. God's plan of salvation is ultimately a paradoxical movement from hardening to the bestowing of mercy: "For God has imprisoned all in disobedience so that he may be merciful to all" (Rom. 11:32).

Questions for Discussion

1. How important has believers' resurrection been in your church? How does resurrection change your understanding of "heaven"?
2. Is it surprising to hear that Paul thinks believers' resurrection is absolutely essential to the faith? Can you think of other "essential" aspects of Christianity that we have tended to ignore?
3. How do you react to Paul's description of Jews and Gentiles in God's plan? What is Paul's primary motivation in taking on this topic?

10

On to Rome

Biblical Texts: Acts 27–28; Philippians; Philemon

Led by God to the Capital of the Empire

Paul's trip by sea to Rome and his two years of house arrest there (61–63 CE; Acts 28:30) form the conclusion of the Acts story of the apostle. His trip from Caesarea probably began in the late summer of 60 CE and ended with his arrival in Rome in the spring of 61. Even as a prisoner, Acts makes it clear that Paul is empowered and led by God: neither shipwrecks (27:13–44) nor snakebites (28:1–6) nor a less-than-enthusiastic Jewish audience (28:23–31) can keep Paul from the bold proclamation in Rome that God has ordained for him (1:8).

Paul's Letters tell us nothing about his treacherous journey to Rome (although see 2 Cor. 11:25–27 for similar earlier experiences), but two of his undisputed letters, Philippians and Philemon, are written from prison, quite probably from Rome.[1] Philippians fits the Roman setting especially well because it describes a man much like the one depicted in Acts 28:16–31, confident in the gospel, even in the face of imprisonment and perhaps death (Phil. 1:20–26).

The well-known "we passages" begin again in Acts 27:1 and continue throughout the sea journey. The details about people, ports, and nautical issues found in this section are impressive. This extensive knowledge about Paul's trip to Rome makes it quite plausible that the writer of these first-person plural sections of Acts is Paul's travel partner.

Sailing for Italy

Shipwrecked

Traveling by ship from Caesarea in Palestine to Rome was no small feat. Because of detours caused by winter winds, Paul traveled at least a thousand miles by sea before finally arriving in Rome. Consult the maps in the back of your Bible to get a sense for the route Paul took. Acts tells us that from Caesarea, Paul traveled north to Sidon (in Syria). Then, fighting the prevailing winds, his ship went around Cyprus and westward along the coast of southern Asia Minor, finally landing in southern Crete at a town named Fair Havens (27:3–8). One of the interesting things about this section of Acts is the authority that Paul is given to advise and lead. With winter weather already upon them, Paul encourages the centurion, pilot, and owner of the ship to stay in Fair Havens (27:10). But they fail to listen to Paul, with disastrous consequences. While trying to reach Phoenix, a good winter port (27:12), they are caught by a strong northeaster and driven into the open sea (27:13–17). After trying various tactics to slow the ship, the sailors finally take desperate measures, throwing cargo and the ship's tackle overboard (28:17–19). Nothing works, and the crew abandons all hope (27:20).

From this point in the story, Paul, a prisoner, assumes leadership on the vessel! Paul shares with everyone a vision he received from an angel of God, affirming that he would witness to the emperor and that all on board would be saved, even though the ship would be lost (27:21–26). God's plan for the proclamation of the gospel cannot be stopped! The apostle stops crew members from deserting the craft (28:31), and he models confident behavior, even encouraging the men to eat before the ship runs aground (28:33–38). The centurion, obviously grateful to Paul, keeps him and the other prisoners from being killed when the ship strikes a reef (28:41–44). All make it safely to land, as Paul's vision had predicted. One is reminded of Old Testament stories where God blesses those whom he has called. Like Joseph and Daniel and others, Paul is noticed even by those who do not share his faith and recognized to be a leader, one whose words must be taken seriously.

Winter in Malta

The Acts story of Paul spending the winter in Malta revolves around two miracle stories that further emphasize Paul's empowerment. While gathering wood for a fire, Paul is bitten by a viper, an extremely poisonous snake (28:1–6). But the snake's bite has no effect on Paul. The natives' opinion of Paul changes from thinking that he must be a criminal (getting his just deserts) to assuming that Paul is a god (compare Paul's experience in Lystra; 14:8–14). As a result, Paul is received and entertained by Publius, a leader of Malta (28:7). He further impresses Publius and his people by healing Publius's father and all the sick brought to him (28:8, 9). The thankful people of Malta provide the ship with the provisions they need for the last leg of the journey (28:10), northward along the western coast of Italy to Rome (28:11–14). Paul may be a prisoner, but as God's apostle he is inevitably distinguished from those around him.

House Arrest in Rome

Once in Rome, Paul is treated well: he is put under house arrest with a guard and is allowed to have guests. Local Christians visit him (28:15), attesting to the fact that the church has been in Rome for some time. Paul also invites Jewish leaders from Rome to meet with him, and it is with these visits and their outcome that Acts concludes its story (28:16–31). Paul's last speech is found in 28:17–22. There he brings these Roman Jews up to speed concerning his arrest and appeal to the emperor. Paul claims that he has done "nothing against our people or the customs" (28:17), noting that even the Roman leaders wanted to release him. We get only the barest hint of the apostle's message about Christ in this setting, but what he says is consistent with his message to Jews elsewhere in Acts: "It is for the sake of the hope of Israel that I am bound with this chain" (28:20). Paul's hearers have heard nothing about him from their friends in Judea, either through letters or through visits, perhaps indicating that even the Jews in Jerusalem realize that Paul is being held on a bogus charge.

Paul's Jewish audience is interested in hearing about the Christian "sect" that is "everywhere . . . spoken against" (28:22). He presents them with the message of Jesus based upon its roots in the Law and the Prophets (28:23), but their response is not overwhelmingly positive. Some believe, while others do not, and they disagree with one another (28:24–25). Paul responds, and thus Acts concludes, with the strongest indictment of Jewish lack of faith to this point. He quotes from Isaiah 6, a passage used elsewhere in the New Testament to explain the Jews' rejection of Christ (Matt. 13:14, 15; Mark 4:12; Luke 8:10):

> For this people's heart has grown dull,
>   and their ears are hard of hearing,
>   and they have shut their eyes;
>   so that they might not look with their eyes,
>   and listen with their ears,
>   and understand with their heart and turn—
>   and I would heal them.

Paul then repeats his now-common affirmation that even though Jews do not hear the gospel, Gentiles will (Acts 28:28):

> Let it be known to you then that this salvation of God has been sent to the Gentiles; they will listen.

This does not mark an end of mission to the Jews. Paul has voiced his frustration at Jewish unbelief before in Acts, yet his approach has almost always been to start with outreach in the synagogue. And Romans 9–11 (see previous chapter) gives a clear overview of how God is leading both Jews and Gentiles to Christ in his plan of salvation. Concluding Acts on this note of Jewish rejection of the gospel may well reflect the situation of the church being addressed by the author of Luke and Acts, however. One of the key themes in Acts is the progression of the gospel from Jews to Gentiles. The author of Acts is addressing a largely Gentile church in the early 80s CE, and Paul's lack of success with the Jews is one way for him to explain the makeup of his own Christian community.

Acts tells us that Paul spends two years in Rome under house arrest, proclaiming the gospel boldly and freely to all who come to him (Acts 28:30–31). I have always felt that Acts ends rather abruptly. What is glaringly absent in the account is an appearance of Paul before the emperor, the essential purpose of Paul's trip to Rome (Acts 27:24), and any indication of how Paul dies. It is hard to believe that if Paul had been able to witness to the emperor that this account would not have been included. Perhaps he was never given an audience with Nero. Writing some twenty years after these events in Rome, the author of Acts surely knew about Paul's death. Early church historian Eusebius says that Paul was executed by Nero in 64 CE, probably at the same time when Peter was killed. Some scholars think that the author of Acts refrains from mentioning Paul's execution in order to preserve a positive attitude toward the Roman government as found throughout this story of the early church. Two ancient documents, *1 Clement* (ca. 95) and the *Muratorian Fragment* (ca. 180), claim that Paul visited Spain before he was executed by Nero.

Paul's Letter Writing in Rome

Philippians

Because of its references to the imperial guard (1:13) and the emperor's household (4:22), many scholars think that Paul's Letter to the Philippians was written while he was imprisoned in Rome. It's one of Paul's most joy-filled letters. In spite of his imprisonment and his possible death (1:20–26; 2:17), he is steadfast in the faith. He recognizes that God's purposes are being served even by his imprisonment (1:12–18). In one unusual section, Paul talks about his death as a good option because he longs "to depart and be with Christ" (1:23). This attitude appears to be a shift from earlier statements where Paul expects to be alive when Christ returns (1 Thess. 4:17). Paul shows deep love for the Philippians in this letter, and certainly his encouragement of them is one of the main reasons for writing.

Although Paul's Letter to the Philippians is not as problem-focused as 1 and 2 Corinthians or Galatians, there are issues in the church he feels called to address. Paul's emphasis upon the need for unity in the church (Phil. 1:27–2:4) may indicate that the congregation does not understand what it means to be *one* in Jesus Christ. He borrows the *kenōsis* (Greek for "emptying") hymn, a liturgical piece commonly used in first-century churches (2:5–11), to show how Jesus Christ models self-giving love. If they are going to practice a love that "looks not to [their] own interests, but to the interests of others" (2:4), they must have the "mind" of Jesus Christ:

> Who, though he was in the form of God,
>   did not count equality with God
>   as something to be exploited,
> but emptied himself,
>   taking the form of a slave,
>   being born in human likeness.
> And being found in human form,
>   he humbled himself
>   and became obedient to the point of death—
>   even death on a cross.

In Philippians 3:2 there is such a radical mood shift that some scholars think 3:2–4:7 may be part of a letter written to Philippi on another occasion. There Paul warns against the "dogs" (3:2), probably a reference to the same sort of Jewish Christians who bothered the Gentiles in Galatia. Paul's defense is one of the most memorable passages in all of his letters. After listing his achievements as a Jew (3:5–6), Paul goes on to say that he considers these things "rubbish" compared to the "surpassing value of knowing Jesus Christ my Lord" (3:7–8). As he might have said in Galatians or Romans, Paul affirms that he has gained a righteousness "not . . . of my own that comes through the law, but one that comes through faith in Christ" (Phil. 3:9).

Paul concludes by encouraging the Philippians with words that sound like they come from an old missionary looking to his heavenly reward. Paul hopes to "attain the resurrection from the dead" (3:11); he looks forward to the "heavenly call of God in Christ Jesus" (3:14). He reminds the citizens of this Roman colony that "our citizenship is in heaven, and it is from there that we are expecting a Savior, the Lord Jesus Christ" (3:20).

Philemon

This short letter was written by Paul from prison (1, 9) to accompany the return of a runaway slave, Onesimus, to his owner Philemon in

Colossae. Although the letter at first appears to be written to Philemon alone, Paul's greetings to others (2) and use of the second-person plural (22) indicate he is writing to a larger group, probably Philemon's house church. In this letter I see a mature Paul, one who both recognizes his power and knows when to curtail it. Paul asks Philemon to take the Christian Onesimus back as a "beloved brother" (16), to forgive this slave of a serious crime. Paul confidently uses his authority as an apostle to encourage Philemon to say yes to this request. Of course, Paul realizes that ultimately the decision must be "voluntary and not something forced" (14), and the most essential imperative he puts upon Philemon is that both he and Onesimus are Christians. As members of the Christian family, where Paul is "father" and Onesimus his "child" (10) and where all three are "brothers" (16, 20), they partake of the new community, where distinctions between slave and free have been left behind (Gal. 3:28). Although abolishing slavery is not a high priority for Paul, probably because he believed Christ would return soon, it is clear that the apostle plants seeds that would make slavery impossible for Christians.

The Pastorals and 2 Thessalonians

For a variety of reasons, most scholars in mainline denominations think that the Pastorals, 1 and 2 Timothy and Titus, were written by followers of Paul after his death. They use language and omit key themes found in the undisputed letters, they appear to address an organized church structure not found in Paul's day, they define women in a way that is not consistent with Paul's undisputed letters, and they appear to assume that Paul visited his churches in Macedonia and Asia Minor *after* his imprisonment in Rome. It is probably best to put 2 Thessalonians in this same category. It appears to copy some of the language and themes of 1 Thessalonians, and it introduces the idea that a "lawless one" (2 Thess. 2:3, 4, 8) must come before Christ returns, quite unlike anything seen in the undisputed letters. Pseudonymous (literally, "false-name") writing, writing in the name of a great thinker or one's teacher, is very common in the ancient world. These pseudonymous writers try to honor Paul's legacy by applying his thought to the church situations of their day. It is essential that

Christian readers not dismiss the Pastorals because they may not have been written by Paul. They too are the inspired, authoritative Word of God, and they too must be used "for training in righteousness" (2 Tim. 3:16).

Colossians and Ephesians

Of these two letters, Colossians is the most likely to have been written by Paul. The author writes from prison (4:4, 18), possibly from Rome. Two names mentioned in Philemon are found here as well (Onesimus and Aristarchus; Col. 4:9–10), and some think the letters may have been delivered together (is Philemon the "letter from Laodicea" mentioned in Col. 4:16?) The church in Colossae was established by Epaphras rather than Paul (1:7; 4:12). This fact and the possibility that it was written by Paul after several years in prison may account for the some of its differences when compared to the undisputed letters. Paul writes to the Colossians to warn them about a heresy unlike any addressed in his other letters. The Christians there have been influenced by what appears to be a form of gnostic[2] Christianity that has legalistic overtones. The Colossians are being deceived by "plausible arguments"; they are taken "captive through philosophy and empty deceit, according to human tradition, according to the elemental spirits of the universe, and not according to Christ" (2:4, 8). Interestingly, the heresy also has a legalistic side. The members of the church at Colossae are being forced to observe "matters of food and drink," "festivals, new moons," and "sabbaths" (2:16). Paul's response to this hybrid, philosophical form of Christianity is to affirm the lordship of Christ in a way that is more powerful than any of his other letters. Read carefully the creedal statement Paul uses in Colossians 1:15–20. There he attests to the preeminence of Christ in relation to all things, creation (15–17), the church (18), and in terms of God's task of reconciliation (19–20). Christ, not philosophical knowledge, is the great mystery of the universe, "in whom are hidden all the treasures of wisdom and knowledge" (2:2–3). Christ is the "head of every ruler and authority" (2:10) and the head of the body, the church (2:19).

Imagine Paul under house arrest in Rome. He hears of a strong challenge to the faith in a church founded by his friend Epaphras, the home church of his fellow disciples Aristarchus and Onesimus. This is a mature Paul, one who has had long days under house arrest to contemplate the faith. He writes his Letter to the Colossians, filled with a joy that is secure even in his imprisonment, confident in the lordship of Christ in spite of challenges in the church, and rising to the challenge of a Christian heresy with Spirit-filled rhetoric. As in Philippians, this is a Paul who is seeing ever more clearly what it means to have been "raised with Christ" (Col. 3:1).

Ephesians is arguably the most theologically sophisticated work in the New Testament. It too claims to be from Paul and while he is in prison (3:1; 4:1). Most scholars in mainline denominations question whether Paul wrote the letter, however. Ephesians seems to be borrowing from other Pauline Letters, particularly Colossians,[3] and the letter does not appear to know specifics about the church at Ephesus (see 1:15 and 3:2). It was probably produced by a Pauline "school" a generation after his death. Again, as in the case of the Pastorals and 2 Thessalonians, it is very important to hear what is being said. Paul probably did not write this letter, but it is authoritative for Christians and has had a huge influence upon Christian thought. One of my favorite passages in all of the New Testament is Ephesians' poetic and beautiful description of the oneness of the church with Christ as its head (4:1–16).

Paul for Today

Christian Joy

What is the basis for the joy you experience in your life? While in prison, Paul is deprived of most of the things that we might list as requisites for a good life. And yet we see in him a joy that many of us would love to experience. Material things appear not to be important to him. Toward the end of Philippians, he speaks about his ability to live with what he has (4:11–13):

For I have learned to be content with whatever I have. I know what it is to have little, and I know what it is to have plenty. In any and all circumstances I have learned the secret of being well-fed and of going hungry, of having plenty and of being in need. I can do all things through him who strengthens me.

The last line is surely the pivotal one. Because of what Paul has in Christ, he is able to live a joy-filled life under house arrest, contemplating execution (Phil. 2:17). Paul even goes so far as to say that meager circumstances and suffering are an important part of the victorious Christian life. Boasting about his weaknesses, the persecutions (2 Cor. 11:23–33) he has suffered, and the physical ailment he has endured (12:7–8), Paul claims that "whenever I am weak, then I am strong" (12:10). It is precisely at those times that he is most aware of the power of Christ working in him (12:9).

Christian Freedom

And it is clear throughout Paul's Letters that freedom is an important component of his joy. He is free from the impossible quest of keeping the law perfectly (Rom. 7:7–25). He is free from the compulsion of salvation through "excellence" or status (Phil. 3:4–11). He is free from worry about the most basic questions of life, whether anything can separate him from God or whether death has power over him (Rom. 8:31–39; 1 Cor. 15:50–58). He is free from legalistic definitions of others that make them enemies or unclean (Gal. 3:28). And Paul has been freed by Jesus Christ *for* love and service. This liberation for others is so complete and wonderful that at times Paul can describe it as a new kind of slavery, to which he can now be fully devoted. Christians are "slaves of righteousness" (Rom. 6:18): "through love," we are to "become slaves to one another" (Gal. 5:13).

Unlike what we are often told, joy and freedom do not come from acquiring things or from claiming our rights, but from knowing that our identity in Jesus Christ liberates us from the burden of self-preservation. The cross turns the world's standards upside down. As Jesus says in the Gospel of Mark, "Those who want to save their life will lose it, and those who lose their life for my sake, and for the sake of the gospel, will save it" (8:35).

Questions for Discussion

1. Name some ways our culture defines joy and freedom that are quite different from Paul's definitions. Why are these definitions often so powerful?
2. When or in what situation does the Christian faith bring you the most joy? Explain why that experience is a joyful one. How is it like or unlike Paul's understanding of Christian joy?
3. As noted above, we as Christians are both free "from" and free "for." Do we tend to emphasize the former more than the latter? In what ways has your faith liberated you "for" something?

11

Paul as a Resource for the Christian Life

Biblical Texts: Romans 5; Ephesians 4; Colossians 1:15–20

This, then, is the witness of Paul to Jesus Christ. On the way to Damascus to find Jewish Christians whom he might imprison, the Pharisee Paul was confronted by the risen Christ. His life is completely and forever changed. The name "Jesus Christ," formerly a blasphemous affront to the oneness of God, now became synonymous with the fullest revelation of God, God's reconciliation of all people. Paul's call to proclaim this message of love propelled him on a thirty-year missionary career. He founded scores of churches in Asia Minor, Macedonia, and Greece and, in the process of dealing with their ongoing problems, first voiced many of the foundational theological and ethical issues of the church.

The study of Paul's life and thought is not easy, but it is immensely rewarding. My hope is that this book will encourage you to continue to study Acts and the apostle's letters. They are a tremendous but underused resource for the Christian life. In the first chapter I spoke of four ways Paul's witness can empower Christians in their experience and practice of the faith. Paul's witness to Jesus Christ tells us that (1) through the life and death of Jesus Christ, God changes us and establishes a new relationship with us; (2) we who are loved by God seek to express our love to others, especially those in the church; (3) people who are transformed through Christ are compelled to share the good news with those around them; and (4) God continues to work in our world to bring salvation to all people.

Is one of these themes especially relevant to your Christian life? One of the wonders of the life and message of Paul is that they resonate with people in various stages of their Christian journey. I never tire of hearing how the God of the universe seeks to reestablish a relationship with his wayward children. Even though we are ingenious in the ways we sin, Paul tells us that "God proves his love for us in that while we still were sinners Christ died for us" (Rom. 5:8). Jesus Christ is God's fullest act of love toward his creation. Everything we do in the Christian faith is a result of this love. Out of joy and thanksgiving, we seek to live lives that are pleasing to God. We love those around us, especially our fellow sisters and brothers in the church. Because salvation comes through Jesus Christ entirely as a gift, we are freed from the burden of "religion" and freed for service. As changed people, both our deeds and words witness to the world about the power of the death and resurrection of Christ.

Perhaps point 4, above, is the most all-inclusive of the teachings in Paul. From a biblical point of view, the history of the world is a story of God seeking fellowship with human beings. When our relationship with God is shattered (Gen. 3), he begins a long-term process of wooing his people back, a plan of salvation that includes the covenants, the law, and the revelations of the biblical writers. But God's most decisive response to human alienation is Jesus Christ. He deals once and for all with Sin and death (Rom. 3:23–26; 1 Cor. 15:20–28). Jesus Christ is the beginning of the last chapter in God's plan for salvation. History has its beginning and end in God. Paul's story, as we have seen, is one small part of this larger drama of salvation. Both Acts and Paul's Letters are acutely aware that God is working in our world, using the gifts of his servants (and even natural and political events) to achieve certain goals. Paul is confident, as he says in Philippians 1:6, "that the one who began a good work among you will bring it to completion by the day of Jesus Christ." Where is God working in your world, involving you in this story of salvation as he involved Paul? Where do you see God's power? Do your prayers reflect the fact that God really acts in our world? What gifts do you have that God "needs" to complete his work here on earth?

One of the most compelling things about Paul is the consistency between what he believes and how he lives. He has come face-to-face with the risen Christ. He believes that God's own Son has entered the world to overcome the barriers that have separated us from God, *and* he allows God to use his life for service. More than any other individual found in the New Testament, Paul models what it means to be a disciple. He shares the message of Christ's resurrection. He loves his fellow Christians and the churches to which they belong. Paul is willing to suffer for the truth of the gospel. He strives to be what he already is in Jesus Christ, a person reconciled to God, a new creation.

As you know, my most basic motivation for writing this book is the desire that Christians, both individually and as communities, might rediscover the power of using Paul as a model. Be open to the transforming vision of the risen Christ, as Paul is. Be ready to live in a way that reflects how God already sees you, as justified people, as adopted children. Paul is not the only powerful example of faith lived, and it is important to find models from various times in history, especially the present. But Paul sets the pace. Among the writers of the New Testament, he is the first and best example of what can happen to people when Christ comes into their lives.

Questions for Discussion

1. Is there one particular event in Paul's life that has been especially helpful in shaping your Christian life? What has its impact been?

2. Do you feel that you know Paul better after this study and after reading the assigned texts? What might be your next step in learning about Paul and having his teachings to be practiced in your church?

3. Is there one particular theological theme in Paul that especially resonates with you? Why does it speak to you? How has learning about it affected your Christian life?

Appendix: A Pauline Chronology

A Chronology of Paul's Life and Undisputed Writings
(All dates are approximate)

5 CE	Paul is born in Tarsus, in Cilicia (Asia Minor)
36	Paul's conversion/call
36–39	Ministry in Nabatea and Damascus
39	Visit to Jerusalem
39–45	Ministry in Cilicia and Antioch
45–50	Paul's first missionary journey
50	Participation in the Jerusalem council
50–52	Paul's second missionary journey
	1 Thessalonians written
52–54	Time spent in Jerusalem and Antioch
54–58	Paul's third missionary journey
	Galatians, 1 and 2 Corinthians, and Romans written
58–60	Paul is arrested in Jerusalem and spends two years in prison in Caesarea
60–61	Paul's sea journey to Rome
61–64	House arrest in Rome
	Philippians and Philemon written
64	Paul is executed in Rome

Notes

Introduction

1. See Frank Thielman, *Theology of the New Testament* (Grand Rapids: Zondervan, 2005), 230–32, for a short discussion of where contemporary scholars see the center of Paul.

2. James C. Howell, *The Beatitudes for Today* (Louisville, KY: Westminster John Knox Press, 2006); Alyce M. McKenzie, *The Parables for Today* (Louisville, KY: Westminster John Knox Press, 2007); and Justo L. González, *The Apostles' Creed for Today* (Louisville, KY: Westminster John Knox Press, 2007).

3. I recommend Raymond Brown, *An Introduction to the New Testament* (New York: Doubleday, 1996); Paul J. Achtemeier, Joel B. Green, and Marianne Meye Thompson, *Introducing the New Testament* (Grand Rapids: Wm. B. Eerdmans Publishing Co., 2001); and Luke Timothy Johnson , *The Writings of the New Testament* (Minneapolis: Fortress Press, 1999).

4. I recommend the *Oxford Annotated Bible* (New York: Oxford, 1994), with comments added to the New Revised Standard Version of the Bible.

5. This phrase has its origin in Albert Schweitzer's famous book, *The Quest of the Historical Jesus*. A good place for laypeople to begin is a book in this series, Ronald J. Allen's *The Life of Jesus for Today* (Louisville, KY: Westminster John Knox Press, 2007).

6. The so-called undisputed letters of Paul, those unquestionably written by him, are Romans, 1 Corinthians, 2 Corinthians, Galatians, Philippians, 1 Thessalonians, and Philemon.

Chapter 2: Paul before His Call

1. Knowing when and in what order Paul wrote his letters is also speculative. Acts 18:12 makes reference to Gallio as proconsul of Achia, and hence Paul's visit to Corinth was ca. 51 CE.

Most scholars, working forward and backward from this date, based
upon the sequence of his career found in Acts and implied in Paul's
Letters, put his conversion/call at about 35 CE.

2.   See, for example, the lists of sins in 1 Cor. 6:9–10 and Rom. 1:29–31.
3.   We will discuss some of these important terms later in the book.

Chapter 3: Paul's Conversion and Call

1.   The Judaism of Paul's day was very much influenced by this movement, as is evidenced by the writings of the Qumran community
and some books found in what we now call the Pseudepigrapha,
2 Baruch, 4 Ezra, and *1 Enoch.* A clear discussion of Jewish apocalypticism and Paul's relationship to it can be found in Calvin J.
Roetzel, *Paul: A Jew on the Margins* (Louisville, KY: Westminster
John Knox Press, 2003), 19–30. A good resource for these and other
Jewish apocalyptic writings is James H. Charlesworth, ed., *The Old
Testament Pseudepigrapha,* vol. 1, *Apocalyptic Literature and Tes-
taments* (New York: Doubleday, 1983).
2.   See the often-quoted "Call Rather Than Conversion" in *Paul among
Jews and Gentiles* (Philadelphia: Fortress Press, 1976), 7–22, for
Krister Stendahl's take on the issue.

Chapter 4: Paul's Early Steps as a Missionary

1.   The various uses of the word "Hellenist" in Acts exemplify the need
for contextual reading.
2.   Perhaps the best discussion of the trip to Arabia and its implications
is found in Jerome Murphy-O'Connor, *Paul: A Critical Life* (New
York: Oxford, 1997), 81–85.
3.   James Frey, *A Million Little Pieces* (London: John Murray Publishers, 2004).
4.   See John Calvin, *Institutes of the Christian Religion,* ed. John T.
McNeill, trans. Ford Lewis Battles, Library of Christian Classics
(Philadelphia: Westminster Press, 1960), 1.8.5.

Chapter 5: The First Missionary Journey

1.   See David J. Bosch, *Transforming Mission: Paradigm Shifts in Theology of Mission* (New York: Orbis Books, 1998), as he addresses
this issue and the one above, on 170–78.
2.   Ibid., 171.

Chapter 6: The Jerusalem Council

1.   A reference is found in 2 Tim. 3:11, but many biblical scholars think
that it was written by a follower of Paul.

2. For an excellent though fairly academic discussion of justification in relationship to the law, see "God's Making Things Right by the Faith of Christ," in J. Louis Martyn, *Galatians* (New York: Doubleday, 1997), 263–75.
3. The same word in Greek is translated in two different ways in most English Bibles: "justification" and "righteousness." In English, "justification" usually refers to an act, while "righteousness" refers to a way of existing.

Chapter 7: Paul's Second Missionary Journey

1. The Egnatian Way in Macedonia was most certainly used by Paul on this trip. Parts of it are still visible today.
2. For this theory, see Raymond Brown, *An Introduction to the New Testament*, 325.
3. That Paul sent Timothy from Athens to Thessalonica appears to be inconsistent with Acts 17:14.
4. Paul prefers to use a shortened version of the name, Prisca, as in Rom. 16:3; 1 Cor. 16:19.
5. Historians date this expulsion at 49 CE. We cannot be sure of the cause, but it is possible that Jews and Jewish Christians were expelled because of conflicts about Christianity.
6. Most probably 2 Corinthians is a compilation of letters written by Paul, at least two and perhaps as many as five.
7. Sheets of papyrus were costly, and private delivery had to be arranged (see Acts 15:22–23).

Chapter 8: Paul's Third Missionary Journey

1. These references to suffering may indicate that Paul was imprisoned in Ephesus. Some scholars think that two books written from prison, Philippians and Philemon, may have been penned at that time.
2. Ephesus was the center for Artemis worship. Its temple to Artemis, a fertility goddess, was considered to be one of the seven wonders of the ancient world.
3. In Rom. 1:17, Paul probably means the phrase "the righteousness of God" to be taken in two ways: (1) how we are made righteous by God, and (2) how God himself is righteous or trustworthy. This later concern surfaces especially in chaps. 9–11.
4. These alliterated terms are the headings for the three sections of the Heidelberg Catechism, said to be based on Romans. The words are also used as a title for a commentary on the catechism edited by Donald J. Bruggink: *Guilt, Grace, and Gratitude: A Commentary on the Heidelberg Catechism Celebrating Its 400th Anniversary* (New York: Half Moon Press, 1963).

5.   See Lyle D. Vander Broek, *Breaking Barriers: 1 Corinthians and Christian Community* (Eugene, OR: Wipf & Stock Publishers, 2007).
6.   George Gallup Jr., *The Unchurched American: 10 Years Later* (Princeton, NJ: Princeton Religion Research Center, 1988).

Chapter 9: Arrested in Jerusalem and Imprisoned in Caesarea

1.   The word "Hebrew" in Acts most probably refers to Aramaic.
2.   Agrippa is the grandson of Herod of the Great. In addition to ruling what had been Philip's region (northeast of Palestine), he rules Galilee as well and has the power to appoint the high priest. Agrippa has Jewish roots.

Chapter 10: On to Rome

1.   Paul's reference to the imperial guard in Phil. 1:13 indicates he was in a Roman prison, but this might have been in Caesarea or Ephesus as well.
2.   Gnosticism became a full-blown Christian heresy in the second century. Perhaps its most essential teaching is that God is far removed from the world and that the world—which is matter—is evil. Because the material world is devalued, the incarnation of Christ is impossible.
3.   At least a third of the verses in Ephesians have direct parallels in Colossians.

Further Reading

Beker, J. Christiaan. *Paul the Apostle: The Triumph of God in Life and Thought.* Philadelphia: Fortress Press, 1980.

Dunn, James D. G., ed. *The Cambridge Companion to St. Paul.* Cambridge Companions to Religion. Cambridge: Cambridge University Press, 2003.

Martyn, J. Louis. *Galatians: A New Translation with Introduction and Commentary.* Anchor Bible 33A. New York: Doubleday, 1997.

Murphy-O'Conner, Jerome. *Paul: A Critical Life.* Oxford: Oxford University Press, 1997.

Reasoner, Mark. *Romans in Full Circle: A History of Interpretation.* Louisville, KY: Westminster John Knox Press, 2005.

Reicke, Bo. *Re-examining Paul's Letters: The History of the Pauline Correspondence.* Edited by David P. Moessner and Ingalisa Reicke. Harrisburg, PA: Trinity Press International, 2001.

Roetzel, Calvin J. *Paul: A Jew on the Margins.* Louisville, KY: Westminster John Knox Press, 2003.

————. *Paul: The Man and the Myth.* Minneapolis: Fortress Press, 1999.

Scroggs, Robin. *Paul for a New Day.* Philadelphia: Fortress Press, 1977.

Vander Broek, Lyle D. *Breaking Barriers: 1 Corinthians and Christian Community.* Eugene, OR: Wipf & Stock Publishers, 2007.

Wiles, Virginia. *Making Sense of Paul: A Basic Introduction to Pauline Theology.* Peabody, MA: Hendrickson Publishers, 2000.